Challenge and Change

History of the Jews in America

Civil War through the Rise of Zionism

Written by: Shelley Kapnek Rosenberg, Ed.D.

Historian and Researcher: Alice L. George, Ph.D.

Historians: Dianne C. Ashton, Ph.D. and Reena Sigman Friedman, Ph.D.

Historical Consultant: Jonathan D. Sarna, Ph.D.

Educational Consultants, Auerbach Central Agency for Jewish Education:
Nancy M. Messinger, Rochelle Buller Rabeeya, and Helene Z. Tigay

Project Directors:
Nancy Isserman
Murray Friedman

This project has been conducted under the auspices of the
Myer and Rosaline Feinstein Center for American Jewish History, Temple University.

BEHRMAN HOUSE, INC.

Designer: Julia Prymak, Pryme Design

Project Editor: Terry Kaye, Behrman House, Inc.

Front Cover Images:

From top left and continuing clockwise: David Ben-Gurion and Golda Meir; A scene in the ghetto, Hester Street 1902; and Private Lewis Leon

Back Cover Images:

From top left and continuing clockwise: Two-dollar Confederate bill with Judah Benjamin portrait, Rebecca Phillips, and a knitting class at the Henry Street Settlement.

Credits:

A scene in the ghetto, Hester Street 1902, B. J. Falk, Library of Congress Prints and Photographs Division, LC-DIG-pan 6a12044 (front cover and p. 3)

Rabbi M. J. Raphall, Library of Congress Prints and Photographs Division, LC-DIG-cph 3b43506 (p. 5)

Rabbi Bernard Illowy, from *Sefer Milchamot Elo-kim,* by Henry Illoway, M. Poppelauer, Berlin, 1914, from the collection of Hebrew Union College-Jewish Institute of Religion, Cincinnati (p. 9)

Sergeant Leopold Karpeles, courtesy of HomeofHeroes.com (p. 11)

Diary of a Tar Heel Soldier, Louis Leon, the frontispiece image, Charlotte, NC, Stone Pub. Co. © 1913, Documenting the American South, The University of North Carolina at Chapel Hill Libraries (front cover and p. 15)

Ezekiel Levy, courtesy of Jacob Rader Marcus Center of the American Jewish Archives, Cincinnati, Ohio (p. 16)

Isaac Levy, courtesy of the Beth Ahabah Museum and Archives Trust, Richmond, Va. (p. 16)

Phoebe Yates Levy Pember and Eugenia Levy Phillips, from the private collection of Robert Rosen (p. 16)

Isaac M. Wise Temple, Library of Congress Prints and Photographs Division, Historic American Buildings Survey Collection, HABS, Ohio, 31-CINT, 12-2 (p. 25)

Galveston immigrants courtesy of the Rosenberg Library, Galveston, Texas (p. 38)

Map of the Pale © 2004 Koret Communications (www.koret.com). All rights reserved. (p. 39)

Floor plan of a tenement, from *How We Lived*, by Irving Howe and Kenneth Libo, copyright © 1979 by Irving Howe and Kenneth Libo. Used by permission of G. P. Putnam's Sons, a division of Penguin Group (USA) Inc. (p. 42)

Portrait of Lillian Wald, Library of Congress, Prints and Photographs Division, Arnold Genthe Collection LC-G412-BN-9448-006 (p. 44)

Knitting class, Henry Street Settlement, New York City, Lewis Wickes Hine, National Child Labor Committee, Library of Congress Prints and Photographs Division, LC-DIG-nclc-04574 (back cover and p. 45)

Work in a sweatshop, Lewis Wickes Hine, National Child Labor Committee, Library of Congress Prints and Photographs Division, LC-DIG-nclc-04076 (p. 51)

Widow and boy rolling papers for cigarettes, Lewis Wickes Hine, National Child Labor Committee, Library of Congress Prints and Photographs Division, LC-DIG-nclc-05349 (p. 53)

Mrs. Finkelstein, with daughters Bessie and Sophie, making garters, Lewis Wickes Hine, National Child Labor Committee, Library of Congress Prints and Photographs Division, LC-DIG-nclc-05348 (p. 53)

Triangle Factory Fire, Kheel Center, Cornell University, Ithaca, N.Y. (p. 55)

Theodor Herzl, courtesy of the Central Zionist Archives, Jerusalem. (p. 60)

Israeli flag ©Photodisc (p. 62)

David Ben-Gurion and Golda Meir, Fritz Cohen, photographer, Israel Government Press Office (front cover and p. 69)

Map of Great Britain's Division of the Mandated Area © 2004 Koret Communications (www.koret.com). All rights reserved. (p. 71)

Posters, courtesy of the Central Zionist Archives, Jerusalem, KRA829 (pioneers) and KRA142 (Keren Kayemet). (p. 72)

Map of the U.N. Partition of Palestine © 2004 Koret Communications (www.koret.com). All rights reserved. (p. 74)

David "Mickey" Marcus, Israel Government Press Office (p. 77)

All other photographs courtesy of American Jewish Historical Society, Newton Center, Massachusetts and New York, New York.

This textbook has been funded by Righteous Persons Foundation, The Farber Foundation, and private donors.

ISBN: 0-87441-778-3
Manufactured in Canada

For additional resources, go to the
Challenge and Change website at
www.challengeandchange.temple.edu.

Contents

Unit 1:
The Civil War and the Jews

CHAPTER 1: **ON THE BRINK OF WAR**   4

CHAPTER 2: **JEWS ON BOTH SIDES**   10

CHAPTER 3: **THE IMPACT OF THE WAR**   18

Unit 2:
Immigration and Labor

CHAPTER 4: **COMING TO AMERICA**   28

CHAPTER 5: **LIFE IN AMERICA**   40

CHAPTER 6: **JEWS IN THE RANKS OF LABOR**   50

Unit 3:
American Jews and Zionism

CHAPTER 7: **THE BEGINNING**   60

CHAPTER 8: **AMERICAN ZIONISM GROWS**   66

CHAPTER 9: **TOWARD STATEHOOD**   70

CHAPTER 1
ON THE BRINK OF WAR

What are the various positions Jews took in the debate on slavery? Why did they take those positions?

When Abraham Lincoln was elected president in 1860, there were about 150,000 Jews living in the United States, about half of 1 percent of the total population, most of whom (about 125,000) lived in the North. The issue of slavery divided the Jewish community, as it did most Americans. Even among the people whose ancestors had fled slavery in Egypt, there were those who argued for the institution of slavery, as well as those who opposed it.

BACKGROUND TO WAR

In the South before the Civil War, Jews of the "upper crust" were well accepted in fashionable society, having lived there for more than a century. Some were even plantation owners who kept slaves and defended what was known as the South's "peculiar institution." The ease with which Jews lived in the South may be seen in these words from a speech delivered by Dr. Jacob de la Motta, a Jewish physician in Charleston, South Carolina, at the dedication of a synagogue in Savannah, Georgia, in 1820. "On what spot in this habitable globe does an Israelite enjoy more blessings, more privileges . . . ? Have we not ample cause to exult?"

In the North, Jews were aware of the importance of preserving the Union and supporting a democracy that had given them opportunities they had never had before. As Myer S. Isaacs wrote in *The Jewish Messenger,* "This Union . . . has been the source of happiness for our ancestors and ourselves. . . . This Republic was the first to recognize our claims to absolute equality, with men of whatever religious denomination." Isaacs's father, Samuel, founded the publication, *The Jewish Messenger,* in 1857.

Among the circumstances that caused the Civil War were major differences in the economies and lifestyles of the Northern and Southern states. Although the North still had many small farms, its economy was becoming more industrial while the South's remained mostly agricultural. Greater demand for cotton by British textile factories and technological advances, especially the invention of the cotton gin in 1793, led to a big increase in cotton production between 1817 and 1860. The South's economy grew slightly faster than the North's between 1840 and 1860, and the wealthiest Southern land owners used enslaved Africans in an effort to make their tobacco and cotton plantations especially profitable. They defended slavery by arguing that it was essential to their cotton-based economy and by claiming that Africans enslaved in the South were better off than free blacks in Africa or the northern United States.

The average white male Southerner, however, was neither a wealthy planter nor a slaveholder. He lived in a cabin and farmed a small patch of land. The proportion of Southern whites who owned slaves had dropped from an all-time high of 40 percent to just 25 percent by 1860. Most Jews were townspeople, not farmers, and so owned few slaves.

While slavery existed in the North in colonial times, it had begun to disappear following the Revolutionary War. In the North, the black population remained small, and whites did not see free blacks as a threat. In the

South, the number of blacks in some places was greater than the number of whites, and slaveholders feared that, if freed, the blacks might seek revenge. In that respect, the attitude of Jewish slaveholders was no different from that of their Christian neighbors.

 Would you expect that being Jewish would make a difference in a person's attitude about a social issue such as slavery? Why? How has being Jewish influenced your opinion about a particular issue?

While **abolitionists** argued that slavery was wrong, they did not agree on how to deal with it. Many abolitionists were Evangelical Protestants who had been involved in efforts to convert Jews. Therefore, even Jews who opposed slavery generally did not identify themselves as abolitionists. In the years leading up to the Civil War, Jewish leaders remained quiet for the most part on the question of slavery, fearing to speak out and believing that silence on this question was in the Jews' best interest.

 Abolitionists are those who fought to abolish slavery.

Rabbi M. J. Raphall

 Watch a portion of the fictionalized miniseries *Roots* (1977) which provides a moving picture of slavery in the United States.

A NORTHERN RABBI'S VIEW OF SLAVERY

To some Jews, slavery was evil. There were also Jews who defended it, however, in both the North and the South. Among those who defended slavery was Morris Jacob Raphall of New York City's Congregation B'nai Jeshurun. An Orthodox rabbi and Bible scholar, Raphall was well-known as the first Jew invited to recite a prayer at an opening session of the U.S. House of Representatives on February 1, 1860. He claimed that, while he was not personally in favor of slavery, the Bible supported it and several examples of slavery could be found in the Biblical text. Raphall gave a sermon on January 4, 1861, to rally public support against the **dissolution** of the Union. Titled "The Bible View of Slavery," the sermon was published and widely distributed by supporters of slavery.

Dissolution of the Union means termination, or ending of the United States as one country.

Raphall wrote: "The result to which the Bible view of slavery leads us is—1st. That slavery has existed since the earliest time; 2d. That slaveholding is no sin, and that slave property is expressly placed under the protection of the Ten Commandments; 3d. That the slave is a person, and has rights not conflicting with the lawful exercise of the rights of his owner. . . ."

Raphall emphasized that the biblical system of slavery was more benevolent than the Southern system, because the Bible saw the slave as a person while Southerners treated slaves as objects. Thus, he believed, Southerners could learn from the biblical approach. Many proslavery Christians also argued that the Bible supported slavery, while people opposed to slavery often used more modern biblical interpretations to support their position.

Can you support the idea that "slaveholding is no sin"? Why does the Torah regulate slavery instead of forbidding it?

 The **Humash** consists of the first five books of the Torah with commentary.

In the *Humash* with commentaries, find the verses from Exodus quoted below. List several points that you would make based on these verses to challenge or support a proslavery opinion.

Write your own review of Rabbi Raphall's speech.

The Ten Commandments: Read them for yourself

Rabbi Raphall quoted the Ten Commandments in his speech. In Exodus 20:8–10, we read: "Remember the Sabbath day to keep it holy. Six days you shall labor and do all your work, but the seventh day is a Sabbath of God: you shall not do any work—you, your son or daughter, your male or female slave." Exodus 20:14 declares: "You shall not covet your neighbor's house: you shall not covet your neighbor's . . . male or female slave . . . or anything that is your neighbor's." [from *JPS Hebrew-English Tanakh: The Traditional Hebrew Text and the New JPS Translation*, 2nd ed. (Philadelphia: Jewish Publication Society, 1999)]

 Covet means "to desire something."

M. J. Raphall's "Bible View of Slavery," reviewed by D. Einhorn (New York, 1861)

In his review, Einhorn wrote:

A religion which exhorts to spare the mother from the bird's nest, cannot consent to the heart-rending spectacle of robbing a human mother of her child. . . . Thus crumbles into a thousand fragments the rickety structure of Dr. Raphall. . . . To proclaim in the name of Judaism, that God has consecrated the institution of slavery! Such a shame and reproach the Jewish religious press is in duty bound to disown and to disavow, if both are not to be stigmatized forever. . . . Why should we . . . keep silence when a Jewish preacher plays such pranks?

Exhort means "to urge" or "to advise."

What do you think of Einhorn's opinion?

Rabbi D. Einhorn

OTHER NORTHERN JEWS SPEAK OUT

Among those who **refuted** Raphall's comments was Michael Heilprin, an encyclopedist and scholar. His lengthy and angry response was published in the antislavery newspaper, *New York Daily Tribune*. He challenged Raphall's historical accuracy and explained that the patriarchs were not slaveowners. Rabbi David Einhorn of Har Sinai Verein in Baltimore was also extremely critical of Rabbi Raphall's opinion. He preached a sermon denouncing Raphall and published reviews of Raphall's speech in his German language periodical *Sinai*. He wrote: "A Jew, the offspring of a race which daily praises God for deliverance from the bondage of Egypt . . . undertakes to parade slavery as a perfectly sinless institution, sanctioned by God . . . ! A more extraordinary phenomenon could hardly be imagined." Einhorn acknowledged that slavery existed in biblical times but believed that the "spirit" of the Bible mandated that it be regulated and eventually abolished.

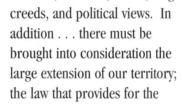 **Refute** means "to counter" or "to rebut."

Ernestine Rose, a staunch American Jewish advocate of women's rights, also spoke out against slavery. She considered it an outrage, and in lectures throughout the Northeast, she supported abolition and other causes that were important to her, such as religious tolerance, public education, and women's rights. She maintained her anti-slavery position even though male slaveholders suggested that they would have tarred and feathered her if she were a man.

On August 4, 1853, in an address in Flushing, New York, celebrating the anniversary of the emancipation of slaves in the British West Indies, Rose said:

"Slavery is not to belong to yourself—to be robbed of yourself. There is nothing that I so much abhor as that single thing—to be robbed of one's self. We are our own legitimate masters. Nature has not created masters and slaves; nature has created man free as the air of heaven. The black man and the white man are equally the children of nature. . . . Humanity's children are, in my estimation, all one and the same family, inheriting the same earth; therefore there

should be no slaves of any kind among them." [from Jacob Rader Marcus, *The American Jewish Woman: A Documentary History* (Cincinnati: KTAV, 1981)]

 Do Jews have a moral obligation to take a stand on social issues like slavery? Why or why not?

A SOUTHERN RABBI'S OPINION

With Abraham Lincoln elected but not yet inaugurated, President James Buchanan proclaimed January 4, 1861, a national fast day on which citizens were to pray for the preservation of the Union. It was on that day that Rabbi Raphall delivered his controversial sermon in New York. At the same time in Baltimore, Rabbi Bernard Illowy preached a sermon at the Lloyd Street Synagogue in favor of secession. The sermon proved so popular among certain Southern Jews that Rabbi Illowy was invited to become the rabbi of Congregation Shaarei Chesed in New Orleans. In his sermon, he said:

"It has ever proved unachievable in a commonwealth to make laws which could meet with the general approval of all its citizens, especially in a Republic like ours, composed of many different nationalities, coming from different countries, differing from each other . . . in customs, manners, habits, languages, creeds, and political views. In addition . . . there must be brought into consideration the large extension of our territory; the law that provides for the

Ernestine Rose

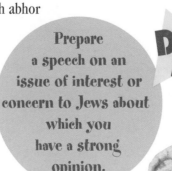 **Prepare** a speech on an issue of interest or concern to Jews about which you have a strong opinion. **DO IT**

benefit of the North, may operate with blighting effect upon the interests of the South, whilst that which promotes the immediate welfare of the South, may be injurious to that of the North. . . .

"Who can blame our brethren of the South for seceding from a society whose government can not, or will not, protect the property rights and privileges of a great portion of the Union against the encroachments of a majority misguided by some influential, ambitious aspirants and selfish politicians who, under the color of religion and the disguise of philanthropy, have thrown the country into a general state of confusion, and millions into want and poverty?"

 Blighting means "destructive."

Encroach is "to interfere gradually." **Encroachment** in this context is the imposition of the ideas, culture, and beliefs of the Northerners on the Southern way of life.

Aspirants are candidates.

The **bimah** is the raised platform in a synagogue from which services are led and the Torah is read.

 Do you think that rabbis should be permitted to speak about political issues from the **bimah**? Have you heard a rabbi do this? If so, what did you think? Do you agree with Rabbi Illowy that the North had no right to attempt to change the practices of the South?

OTHER SOUTHERN JEWS TAKE A STAND

Many Jews, like other Americans, were torn between supporting their state and supporting the country as a whole. One explanation for what might seem to have been an odd choice for Jews to make—supporting the South with its institution of slavery—comes from a man named Joseph Goldsmith, who was connected with the War and Navy Departments of the Confederacy as a contractor for weapons. After the war, he wrote:

"I am still a living witness and can, from my own memory, give you many names of gallant Jewish soldiers of the Confederate Army I had ample opportunity to see

and to know. . . . And I know further that it was simply a sense of loyalty to their homes and their neighbors that prompted them to fight for the South. If not, they could readily have left this country at any time as I myself could have done, had I so chosen. But love for our adopted country kept us here and we offered all we had in its behalf." [from Simon Wolf, *The American Jew as Patriot, Soldier, and Citizen* ed. Louis Edward Levy (Philadelphia: Levytype, 1895)]

Captain David Camden De Leon, a member of a large South Carolina Sephardic family and a surgeon in the U.S. Army, was known as the "Fighting Doctor" for his bravery during the Mexican War. At the beginning of the Civil War, he had not decided which side to support. In a letter to his brother Edwin, he wrote: "Treason and patriotism are next door neighbors and only accident makes you strike the right knocker. . . . I have loved my country, I have fought under its flag, and every star and stripe is dear to me. . . . But I am still convinced that no man can be a patriot who is afraid of being thought a traitor." Although he did not approve of secession, he resigned from the Union army and joined the Confederate forces as surgeon general in charge of organizing their entire medical department.

Edwin De Leon, David's older brother, was a lawyer and a journalist who favored slavery. Before the war, he had been consul general for Egypt. When South Carolina seceded from the Union, he faced a dilemma similar to his brother's. He, too, resigned his position and offered his services to the Confederacy. Jefferson Davis appointed him as his personal envoy to Europe, hoping that De Leon would convince France and England to recognize the Confederacy. Those countries would not support a slaveholding nation, however, and De Leon failed to convince them of the correctness of this position.

 An **envoy** is a representative or messenger.

 Southerners in the U.S. Army or in government service faced a difficult decision: Should they remain loyal to the Union and fight against residents of their home state, or should they side with their state? What would you have done? Why?

Did any of your ancestors fight in the Civil War? Go to www.jewish-history.com/civilwar.htm to check out the "Jewish Civil War Veterans database."

THE WAR BEGINS

Many in the South considered Lincoln a strong opponent of slavery and South Carolina left the Union six weeks after his election. By February 1861, six more Southern states—Alabama, Florida, Georgia, Louisiana, Mississippi, and Texas—had seceded from the Union. They sent representatives to Montgomery, Alabama, to form their own government—the Confederate States of America.

Jefferson Davis, having been elected president of the Confederacy, ordered the Confederate general P. G. T. Beauregard to demand the surrender of the Northern troops stationed at Fort Sumter in the Charleston, South Carolina harbor. Beauregard ordered his men to open fire on the fort on April 12, 1861, thus beginning open warfare. After Lincoln ordered state militias to end the rebellion, Arkansas, North Carolina, Tennessee, and Virginia joined the Confederacy.

 To **secede** meant to break away or to withdraw from the United States to form a new country.

THINK ABOUT IT In your opinion, why did most Jewish leaders believe it was in the Jews' best interest to remain silent about slavery? Do you think that was the right decision?

Rabbi Bernard Illowy

Jews Support One Another

Despite their differences, Jews supported other Jews. Isaac Mayer Wise offered support for Jewish Confederate prisoners of war, attempting unsuccessfully to gain their release and publishing their names in his newspaper in order to locate their relatives and get food packages delivered to them. Many Northern Jewish communities responded to Southern requests for aid. In 1865, after Savannah had surrendered to Union troops, its Jewish community pleaded with the Northern newspaper editors Isaac Leeser and Samuel Isaacs for matzot for Passover. In response, New York Jews donated 3,000 pounds of matzot and Philadelphia Jews donated 2,000 pounds. Wise and Leeser visited Richmond after the war, gave sermons there, and were distressed by the suffering of the city's Jewish community. And throughout the war, B'nai B'rith continued to function as a national Jewish fraternal organization.

DO IT List some ways in which Jews support other Jews today.

_____

_____

_____

_____

_____

_____

_____

_____

CHAPTER 2
JEWS ON BOTH SIDES

What roles did Jews play in supporting the North and the South?
How did their religion shape the experiences of Jewish soldiers in the Union and Confederate armies?

Life was generally good for Jews in America before the Civil War. Although their acceptance by their fellow citizens was somewhat limited, antisemitism was largely dormant. Once war came, Jews were loyal to the section of the country in which they lived: In the North, they strongly supported the Union while in the South they supported the Confederacy. But the war divided American Jewish families just as it divided other American families. In one family, four children fought for the South while one fought for the North. In another, a brother died for the Southern cause and a husband was wounded fighting for the North.

Between 8,000 and 10,000 Jews fought on one side or the other during the Civil War. Most were volunteers who enlisted as privates; at least fifty of them rose through the ranks to become officers.

Dormant means "inactive, hidden." Signs of antisemitism were hidden from public view during the pre-Civil War period.

JEWS FIGHT FOR THE UNION

Although Jews had not been allowed to serve in the military throughout most of European history, they had played a role in the defense of their communities in North America since the 1600s. At least 6,000 Jews served in the Union army, and six received the Congressional Medal of Honor, the nation's highest military award for bravery.

Two brothers, Joseph and Marcus Spiegel, immigrants from Germany, served in the Ohio Volunteers, and Marcus rose to the rank of colonel before his death from battle wounds in 1864. Charles Etting of Baltimore trained as a cadet at West Point before serving in the Union army. His cousin Cary Gist Gratz of Lexington, Kentucky, was killed defending the Union at the battle of Wilson's Creek.

Edward Rosewater was a member of the Telegraphers Corps of the Union army. Originally stationed in the South, he moved north and enlisted when war broke out. After serving first in West Virginia and then Virginia, he was transferred to the War Department in Washington, D.C., where Lincoln would come to his office to read dispatches from the troops. On January 1, 1863, he was the telegraph operator who spread word of the Emancipation Proclamation.

Jewish doctors served in both the Union army and navy. Dr. Nathan Mayer joined the army as an assistant surgeon in a Connecticut regiment of volunteers. He soon became a full surgeon and served at many of the most important battles of the war. At Antietam, he used a farmhouse as a field hospital where he had some success using chloroform, an early anesthetic. Captured with his regiment, he was held for seven months. After his release, he was sent to a hospital in North Carolina, where he caught yellow fever. The epidemic killed eighteen of his medical assistants, and Mayer himself returned to the operating room before he had completely recovered. Since the typical medication, quinine, was not successful, he treated himself and others with calomel and castor oil with much better results. By the war's end, he was a brigadier general in charge of the military stores in eastern North Carolina.

Calomel is a white tasteless powder used as a medication.

Sergeant Leopold Karpeles, born in Prague in Central Europe and raised in Texas, is one of six Jewish Civil War soldiers known to have received the Congressional Medal of Honor. He was a member of the Fifty-seventh Massachusetts Infantry, which came under fire during a three-day battle in Virginia. The battle was important: The Union's General Ulysses S. Grant had intended it to serve as the first step toward capturing Richmond. As a "color sergeant," Karpeles held the only Union flag that could be seen on the battlefield as General James Wadsworth rode along the lines, encouraging his soldiers to hold off the Confederate attack. They did, and

Karpeles was rewarded for his bravery. He took part in many other battles and was wounded several times. Later he became a founding member of the Medal of Honor Legion.

List the names of other Jews who have received the Congressional Medal of Honor and the reasons why they were honored.

DO IT

_____

_____

_____

_____

_____

_____

_____

_____

_____

_____

_____

_____

_____

The Medal of Honor

The Medal of Honor is presented in the name of the U.S. Congress for heroic actions against an enemy force. It was first presented during the Civil War in 1863.

THINK ABOUT IT

Why is it important that American Jews have received this honor?

_____

Sergeant Leopold Karpeles

The Jewish American Hall of Fame

Leopold Karpeles's bravery has been remembered with a medal marking his admission to the Jewish-American Hall of Fame. One side shows Karpeles with the flag. The reverse depicts a letter from President Lincoln to Mikveh Israel in Philadelphia thanking the congregation for its prayers. Among the other honorees of the Jewish-American Hall of Fame are physicist Albert Einstein, microbiologist Jonas Salk, and composer George Gershwin.

CLICK ON IT

You can see the Jewish-American Hall of Fame medals at www.amuseum.org/jahf.

Visit the website, and nominate a Jewish person to the Hall of Fame. It may be someone famous who is not already listed or someone who is not famous but you believe should be recognized. Create a medal for your nominee.

DO IT

JEWISH SOLDIERS IN THE UNION ARMY PRAY TOGETHER

With the war underway, Northerners and Southerners believed that military success would be linked to the piety of their own region and the soldiers who defended it. It was common for Jewish soldiers in the same company to pray together on Shabbat. Others expressed their religious beliefs in other ways. One young soldier fought on Yom Kippur morning without having eaten. As soon as the enemy retreated, he went to the woods alone and remained there reading prayers until sundown.

Sometimes, however, Jews had to fight for the right to maintain their own traditions. In 1862, in a letter to President Lincoln that was published in *The Occident,* the father of a Union soldier protested an order that Union soldiers "observe the Sabbath and do no work on Sunday, because we are a Christian people." Reminding Lincoln of the Declaration of Independence and the Constitution, the letter writer, B. Behrend of Sullivan County, New York, declared that "the people of the United States is not a Christian people, but a free, sovereign people with equal rights." He pointed out that "each and every citizen of the United States has the right and liberty to live according to his own consciousness in religious matters, and no one religious denomination, be it a majority or minority of the people, can have a privilege before the other under this our beloved Constitution."

LEARN IT

Sovereign means "independent."

Behrend asked the president, "to make provision, and to proclaim in another order, that also all those in the army who celebrate another day as the Sunday may be allowed to celebrate that day which they think is the right day according to their own conscience." He concluded by saying, "I gave my consent to my son, who was yet a minor, that he should enlist in the United States army; I thought it was his duty, and I gave him my advice to fulfill his duty as a good citizen, and he has done so. At the same time I taught him also to observe the Sabbath on Saturday. . . . Now I do not want that he shall be dragged either to the stake or the church to observe the Sunday as a Sabbath. . . . I love my country, the Constitution, and the Union, and I try to be always a loyal citizen."

THINK ABOUT IT Why is it important for Jews to speak out the way Behrend did? Have you ever spoken out in a similar way?

Some Jewish soldiers suggested that they be organized into Jewish regiments, with Hebrew banners, so that they could maintain a kosher diet and fulfill their other religious obligations. That proposal was not approved. As one Jewish soldier wrote, "We are quite satisfied to fight with our Christian comrades for one cause, one country, and *the Union.*" According to historians, however, there were a few special Jewish companies, such as the Eighty-second Illinois Volunteer Infantry. Though other companies had large numbers of Jewish soldiers, they were not completely Jewish.

A special Passover

A group of Jewish soldiers in the Union army celebrated Passover together in a notable way. J. A. Joel, stationed in West Virginia, wrote about it in *The Jewish Messenger* **in 1866:**

Being apprised of the approaching Feast of Passover, twenty of my comrades and co-religionists belonging to the Regiment, united in a request to our commanding officer for relief from duty, in order that we might keep the holydays, which he readily acceded to. . . . Our next business was to find some suitable person to proceed to Cincinnati, Ohio, to buy us Matzos. Our sutler *being a co-religionist and going home to that city, readily undertook to send them. We were anxiously awaiting to receive our matzos and about the middle of the morning of Erev Pesach a supply train arrived in camp, and to our delight seven barrels of Matzos. On opening them, we were surprised and pleased to find that our thoughtful sutler had enclosed two* Hagedahs *and prayer-books. We were now able to keep the seder nights, if we could only obtain the other requisites for that occasion. We held a consultation and decided to send parties to* forage *in the country while a party stayed to build a log hut for the services. About the middle of the afternoon the foragers arrived, having been quite successful. We obtained two kegs of cider, a lamb, several chickens and some eggs. Horseradish or parsley we could not obtain, but . . . we found a weed, whose bitterness . . . exceeded anything our forefathers "enjoyed." . . . The necessaries for the* choroutzes *we could not obtain, so we got a brick*

which, rather hard to digest, reminded us, by looking at it, for what purpose it was intended.

At dark we had all prepared, and were ready to commence the service. . . . The ceremonies were passing off nicely, until we arrived at the part where the bitter herb was to be taken. We all had a large portion of the herb ready to eat at the moment I said the blessing; each ate his portion, when horrors! what a scene ensued in our little congregation, it is impossible for my pen to describe. The herb was very bitter and very fiery like Cayenne pepper, and excited our thirst to such a degree, that we forgot the law authorizing us to drink only four cups, and the consequence was we drank up all the cider. Those that drank the more freely became excited, and one thought he was Moses, another Aaron, and one had the audacity to call himself Pharaoh. . . .

LEARN IT

A **sutler** is a merchant who sells goods to an army.

Forage means to go in search of supplies.

Choroutzes is an old-fashioned spelling of *haroset*, the mixture of fruit, nuts, and wine that is put on the seder plate as a symbol of the bricks that Israelite slaves were forced to haul to build the pyramids in Egypt.

CLICK ON IT To read more about this Union soldier's Passover celebration, go to www.jewish-history.com/civilwar.htm, and click on "Union Soldiers Passover Seder."

Lieutenant Colonel Edward S. Salomon commanded the Eighty-second, which included more than one hundred Jews, during the monumental three-day Battle of Gettysburg. Salomon had come to America from Germany in his teens and had held a variety of jobs before studying law. He enlisted at the start of the war and saw action in several battles. He was said to have displayed "the highest order of coolness and determination under very trying circumstances" at Gettysburg. He received a commendation for his bravery and was promoted to the rank of brigadier general. At the close of the war, he led his men in a parade in Washington, D.C., and in 1870, President Grant appointed him governor of Washington Territory.

CLICK ON IT

Read more about this Jewish regiment. Go to www.geocities.com/Athens/Parthenon/7419.

DO IT

List arguments for and against the idea of Jewish regiments.

NORTHERNERS OFFER SUPPORT ON THE HOME FRONT

Jews who did not join the military supported the troops from home. Families contributed money to the war effort, and many Jewish women worked in hospitals, sewed clothes, made bandages, and collected money for soldiers' families and others in need. Some Jewish organizations helped the families of Jewish soldiers, while others offered help to anyone who needed it. Jewish women's groups played an important role in the war effort, along with similar groups run by women in the Christian community. Such groups participated in fund raising fairs organized by the U.S. Sanitary Commission, which coordinated fund raising and the distribution of supplies nationwide during the war.

Many Jewish women living near Union infirmaries resisted the social customs that barred them from working in hospitals and volunteered to nurse wounded soldiers. Soldiers benefiting from their aid were twice as likely to recover and survive their wounds as were soldiers nursed by men.

The Ladies' Hebrew Association for the Relief of Sick and Wounded Union Soldiers was organized in Philadelphia in 1863 as a result of an exchange of letters between Reverend Sabato Morais of Mikveh Israel and Mary Rose Smith, head of the women's division of the U.S. Sanitary Commission in Philadelphia. In a sermon explaining the importance of organizing a women's war-relief society, Reverend Morais said: "While we dwell here securely, in the fruition of God's bounty, thousands of our fellow-beings are exposed to dangers and privations. . . . Charity—the handmaid of religion—can soften their pangs. I would urge the ladies of my persuasion to join hands with their sisters of a different creed in the discharge of a philanthropic task."

According to the *Philadelphia Public Ledger,* the Ladies' Hebrew Association was to provide "sick and wounded soldiers, irrespective to religious creed . . . with delicacies and clothing while they lie in the army hospitals." In 1865, the Association reported that it had sent ten crates of supplies to the Sanitary Commission during the previous year. [from Bertram Korn, *American Jewry and the Civil War* (New York: Atheneum, 1970)]

THINK ABOUT IT

Why was it important that Jewish women volunteered to support the war effort?

On every possible occasion, Jews raised money for the war. Appeals were made from synagogue pulpits on holidays, and refreshments were sold for the benefit of the Sanitary Commission at community events. One of Rabbi David Einhorn's patriotic sermons was printed and sold, with the profits donated to the commission. No precise records were kept of the amounts of the donations, but it is evident that the Jewish community worked hard to fulfill its obligation.

At the beginning of the war, the effort to raise money was hindered because Union bonds could not be sold in foreign countries. Europeans considered Confederate bonds more valuable because of the South's cotton trade with England. In response to the Union's financial difficulties, a Jewish family by the name of Seligman engaged the services of its international banking firm, J. and W. Seligman and Company. The branch of the family's bank in Frankfurt, Germany, sold more than $200 million in Union bonds, and all the company's branches became agents for the sale of U.S. bonds. In addition, the Union owed the family more than $1 million for clothing bought on credit from its dry-goods business. Contributions like these led President Lincoln to say, "No class of citizenship in the United States was superior in patriotism to those of the Jewish faith."

Bonds are certificates of debt issued by a government or a corporation with the promise of repaying the debt, usually at a fixed rate of interest.

SOUTHERN JEWISH SOLDIERS MAINTAIN THEIR JUDAISM

At least 1,200 Jewish soldiers fought for the Confederate forces, and at least twenty-one were staff officers. One of them, Major Raphael Jacob Moses, a member of General James Longstreet's staff, sat at General Robert E. Lee's dinner table. As the officer in charge of provisions and supplies for the state of Georgia, he carried out the last order of the Confederacy, delivering $10,000 in **bullion** to be used to feed returning soldiers and to care for the wounded in hospitals.

Bullion is gold or silver formed into bars.

Jewish soldiers in the Confederate army attempted to maintain their traditions, even in the midst of war. Private Isaac Gleitzman of Arkansas, for example, was said to have carried two mess kits: one for dairy products and one for meat.

Rabbi Maximilian Michelbacher of Congregation Beth Ahabah in Richmond, Virginia, requested that General Lee permit Jewish soldiers to leave the front lines in order to celebrate the High Holidays in

Richmond. Lee responded saying that he wished that he could grant the request, but such a leave would jeopardize the cause. He added, "Should any be deprived of the opportunity of offering up their prayers according to the rites of their Church that their penitence may nevertheless be accepted by the Most High, & their petitions answered."

By 1862, conditions had changed. A Private Lewis Leon wrote in his journal: "Sept 19—This morning they read an order from our father R. E. Lee in which he gave furlough into Richmond of all Israelites in honor of the Jewish New Year. Wortheim, Oppenheim, Norment, Katz, and myself, as well as Lt. E. Cohen worshipped." [from Lewis Leon, "Diary of a Confederate Soldier," in Morris Schappes, *A Documentary History of the Jews in the United States 1654–1875* (NY: Schocken Books, 1971)]

Even when Jewish soldiers could not leave their regiments, they attempted to worship together. In a letter to his sister, Leonora, explaining how he and their brother Ezekiel observed Passover, Isaac J. Levy, of the Forty-sixth Virginia Infantry, wrote, "We were all under the impression in camp that the first day of the festival was the 22nd . . . Zeke was somewhat astonished . . . to learn that that was the first Seder night. He purchased Matzot sufficient to last us for the week. The cost is somewhat less than in Richmond, being but two dollars per pound.

Private Lewis Leon

Ezekiel Levy

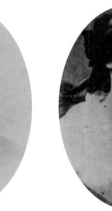

Isaac Levy

Phoebe Yates Levy Pember

Eugenia Levy Phillips

"We are observing the festival in a truly Orthodox style. On the first day we had a fine vegetable soup. It was made of a bunch of vegetables which Zeke brought from Charleston containing new onions, parsley, carrots, turnips, and a young cauliflower, also a pound and a half of fresh [kosher] beef, the latter article sells for four dollars per pound in Charleston. Zeke E. . . . brought some of his own, smoked meat, which he is sharing with us. . . ."

Read more about this Southern soldier's Passover. Go to www.jewish-history.com/civilwar.htm and click on "Jews in the Civil War" and then "Confederate Soldiers Passover Seder."

THINK ABOUT IT

Do you believe it is important for a Jewish soldier to attempt to observe religious rituals and customs during wartime? Why? Is there one tradition that you would observe?

SOUTHERN JEWS SUPPORT THE SOUTH

Jews supported the South in a variety of ways. For example, Benjamin Mordecai contributed $10,000 to the cause. After investing all his money in Confederate bonds, he died a poor man. Phoebe Yates Levy Pember, a widow from Georgia who had moved to Richmond, served as head matron of that city's Chimborazo Military Hospital, then the largest military hospital in the world. Her job was to care for the wounded. She also supervised the diet of the troops

and was known for serving them chicken soup. She was the first woman to hold so responsible a position at Chimborazo.

Rosanna Dyer Osterman had helped her husband start a business in Galveston, Texas. When the war started, military forces blockaded the city, and many residents were evacuated. Nonetheless, Osterman stayed to nurse the sick and wounded. When Galveston fell to the Union, she carried military information to Confederate officials in Houston, helping the Southern forces retake the city on New Year's Day 1863. Osterman died in the explosion of a steamboat on the Mississippi River when she was fifty-seven years old. In her will, she left money to support Jewish hospitals around the country and to establish the Hebrew Benevolent Society in Galveston to aid sick and poor people of all religions.

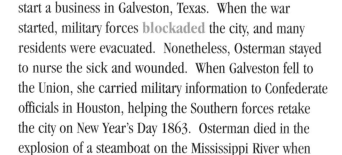

During a **blockade**, ships or soldiers cut off access to an area.

On two occasions, Union authorities arrested Eugenia Levy Phillips, the sister of Phoebe Yates Levy Pember and a third generation Southerner who was married to Philip Phillips, a prominent attorney. In 1861, the Phillipses were living in Washington, D.C. In August of that year, Eugenia was accused of spying for the Confederacy and was held with her sister and daughters in the attic of a local house. Her husband was arrested as well and held under house arrest for a week before being cleared of the charges. After three weeks, Eugenia was released and the family left for New Orleans. When they passed through Richmond, the capital of the Confederacy, President Jefferson Davis and his wife entertained them. It was rumored that Eugenia Phillips carried a coded message to Davis in a ball of yarn.

She later drew Union officers' wrath in New Orleans for encouraging her children to spit on Union soldiers, an act she eventually apologized for. Then, in 1862, she was seen on her balcony "laughing and mocking" the body of a Union soldier during a funeral procession. General Benjamin Butler imprisoned her again, this time on Ship Island, Mississippi. Phillips was allowed one servant, received a soldier's daily ration which consisted mainly of spoiled beef and beans, and was allowed to communicate only through Butler's office. She was released after several months, after much uproar across the South about her treatment, and given the choice of taking the loyalty oath or declaring that she was an enemy of the United States. She would not take the oath, and she and her family took a small boat and went to Georgia. Eugenia Levy Phillips's journal, kept between 1861 and 1862, is among her family's papers at the Library of Congress.

Go to www.jewish-history.com.htm and click on "Jews in the Civil War" and "Eugenia Phillips and General Butler: 'Beauty and the Beast'" to read the journal.

What is your opinion of Jewish support for the Southern cause?

SOUTHERN JEWS WITH MIXED FEELINGS

Philip Phillips, Eugenia's husband, had long opposed secession. Despite his wife's support for the South, he would not support the Confederacy. However, as a Southerner, he would not work for the Union. After the war, the family returned to Washington where Phillips argued cases before the U.S. Supreme Court, becoming one of the most successful lawyers in the country.

Solomon Heydenfeldt, a county judge in Mobile, had let the governor know that he favored an amendment to the Alabama state constitution that would prohibit bringing more slaves into the state. He moved to San Francisco in 1850, where he served as an associate justice of the California Supreme Court. He believed in states' rights and thought that the South should eliminate slavery of its own accord, without interference from the federal government. He wished to see the Union preserved, but opposed the use of force. Similarly, he opposed slavery, but supported the Confederacy.

What do you think of Southern Jews who did not support the Confederacy?

OTHER DIVISIONS

Even in their prayers, Jews found themselves divided. Southern rabbis asked God to support the South in the war. For example, Reverend Maximilian Michelbacher of Richmond, wrote, "a menacing enemy is arrayed against the rights, liberties, and freedom of this, our Confederacy . . . Here I stand now with many thousands of the sons of the sunny South, to face the foe, to drive him back, and to defend our natural rights. O Lord, God of Israel, be with me. . . ." In New Orleans, Reverend James Gutheim prayed that "the unrighteous invaders be repulsed on every side . . ."

Northern rabbis prayed for the reestablishment of the Union. A prayer by Reverend Sabato Morais asked God to make Southerners once again loyal to the United States.

DO IT Write a prayer that expresses your feelings about war or slavery and freedom.

_____

_____

_____

_____

_____

_____

_____

_____

_____

_____

CHAPTER 3

THE IMPACT OF THE WAR

What was the impact of the Civil War on Jews in the North and the South?

Like other Americans, Jews in the North and the South suffered greatly during the war. The loss of life on both sides was staggering, and many families lost their homes and their businesses. Latent antisemitism, which had existed since the founding of the country, gave way to open hatred of Jews during the war, and these sentiments persisted in various ways into the postwar years. Nevertheless, Jews were proud of their military, philanthropic, and other personal contributions to the war effort and felt themselves more a part of the country than before.

Latent means "concealed" or "dormant."

ANTISEMITISM GROWS IN AMERICA

Although Jews often proclaimed their love for their country and their willingness to support it, significant anti-Jewish feelings surfaced as a result of wartime tensions. Jews on both sides were accused of being disloyal, lacking patriotism, and profiting financially from the war. On the Union side, they were accused of gold speculation, smuggling and trading illegally with the Confederacy, and providing the enemy with supplies. Jewish bankers often became the targets of attacks. Among these were August Belmont, who had no connections to the Jewish community, and the Seligman brothers, who sold Union bonds to support the war effort. Some Union propaganda was religious, attacking Jews simply for being non-Christians.

Because many Jews in Southern towns were shopkeepers, they sometimes fared better than others in their communities during the war, and those who suffered economically often envied them. With supplies scarce and prices climbing, some gentiles blamed the South's problems on the Jews. A grand jury in Talbotton, Georgia, concluded that high prices were

the Jews' fault and passed a resolution condemning them for their "evil and unpatriotic conduct." The family of Lazarus Straus, the only Jewish family in town, owned a store and had contracts to buy supplies for the Confederate government. When the resolution passed, they moved away. After the war, Straus took his family north.

In the chaotic postwar Southern economy, cotton was not being shipped. Some Straus money was invested in cotton and the family consequently faced financial difficulties. Nevertheless, Straus paid his debts. Twenty-eight years later, when his son Isidor applied to the United States Trust

The Abraham and Straus delivery wagons.

Company for a business loan, the father's fine reputation served as the necessary assurance that the son would repay the loan. Isidor's business would become Abraham and Straus, a major department store. In 1896, Isidor and his brother Nathan took over R. H. Macy which, at one time, was the largest department store in the world.

THE CHAPLAINCY ISSUE

Even though religious rights for all Americans are guaranteed by the Bill of Rights, only Protestant ministers were permitted to serve as military chaplains before the Civil War. At the beginning of the war, Congress passed a law permitting any "regularly ordained minister of some Christian denomination" to become a chaplain. That meant that Protestant ministers and Catholic priests could be chaplains, but rabbis could not. Congress rejected a proposal to expand the wording to allow rabbis to serve. The Confederacy allowed any "clergyman" to serve as a chaplain, but because there were so few Jews in any given Confederate regiment, the Confederate government saw no need for a Jewish chaplain.

THINK ABOUT IT Why was it important that Jews be allowed to serve as chaplains?

The Sixty-fifth Regiment of the Fifth Pennsylvania Cavalry was commanded by Colonel Max Friedman, a Jew, and had a large number of Jewish members. Michael Allen, a Jewish layman and Hebrew teacher, was appointed the regiment's chaplain. The Young Men's Christian Association (YMCA), which was responsible for supervising military chaplains in the Union army considered Allen unqualified to serve as a chaplain because he was neither Christian nor an ordained rabbi, and the organization forced his resignation.

After many petitions and protests, in 1862, Congress agreed to reinterpreted the original law to allow any "regularly ordained minister" to serve as chaplain. Ultimately, two Jewish chaplains served Union troops: Jacob Frankel became the first American rabbi appointed to the position of military hospital chaplain, and Reverend Ferdinand Leopold Sarner became the first Jewish regimental chaplain, of the Fifty-fourth New York Volunteer Infantry.

DO IT Find out about rabbis serving as chaplains in the U. S. military today. How do their duties compare with those of a pulpit rabbi? In recent years, some women have become the military's first female Jewish chaplains. Have they faced discrimination in the Armed Forces?

THE JEWISH "BRAINS OF THE CONFEDERACY"

While Southern Jews supported the Confederacy in many ways, the one Jew who is most often identified with the Confederate cause is Judah Benjamin, an important member of Jefferson Davis's cabinet. Benjamin had great influence, but was also the target of much anti-Jewish hostility in both the North and the South. Some Southerners tended to blame him for all the Confederacy's problems, especially its military defeats.

Judah Philip Benjamin was born in the West Indies in 1811 and raised in Charleston. After attending Yale College, he began a successful law practice in New Orleans. President Franklin Pierce wished to nominate him as a candidate for Supreme Court justice, a post Benjamin refused.

Benjamin bought a sugar plantation in Louisiana and experimented with methods of extracting and refining sugar. He owned 140 slaves until 1850, when he sold the plantation. He was a founder of the Illinois Central Railroad, was elected to both houses of the Louisiana State Assembly, participated in the state's constitutional convention, and was elected to the U.S. Senate from Louisiana in 1852.

While in the Senate, Benjamin was recognized for his speeches on the legal basis for slavery and the constitutional grounds of states' rights. On February 4, 1861, in a farewell speech in the Senate, he defended the right of the Southern states to secede.

When the Confederacy was formed, Jefferson Davis appointed Benjamin attorney general and he soon became Davis's close friend and trusted adviser. When the secretary of war resigned, Davis named Benjamin to succeed him. At first, Benjamin's efforts to increase the size of the army and the amount of supplies led Southerners to approve of his work. But he lacked military knowledge and experience, and soon he encountered difficulties in his dealings with Generals Robert E. Lee, T. J. Jackson, and P. G. T. Beauregard.

Compounding Benjamin's problems was the fact that Davis, who had been secretary of war in Pierce's cabinet, wanted control of the army. After the capture of Fort Donelson in Tennessee and the loss of Roanoke Island, North Carolina, to the Union forces in 1862, he accepted the blame and resigned even though the decision to give up the island had been made by Davis. There were vicious attacks on "Judas Iscariot Benjamin" for his refusal to send more men and guns to the fort. The truth was that there was nothing to send and Benjamin did not want to reveal the truth to the enemy. Nevertheless, there was criticism of him. Rabbi Maximilian Michelbacher said that Benjamin was attacked so that those "actually guilty could escape punishment."

Davis then appointed Benjamin secretary of state in the hope that he would persuade the European countries to recognize the Confederacy and lift their blockade. Benjamin, believing that such recognition would promote the peace process and end the war, attempted a variety of strategies, including the threat of restricting commerce with any country that refused to recognize the South. He also tried to win over European businessmen who bought Southern goods and might influence their governments on the Confederacy's behalf. He even suggested that the South's slaves be freed. None of his efforts succeeded, and some Southerners claimed that he had transferred Confederate funds to his personal bank accounts in Europe.

After Lee's surrender and Lincoln's assassination, Benjamin was one of the Confederate officials suspected of plotting the assassination. He fled to England, convinced that antisemitism, as well as the Union's anger at the Confederacy, would make it impossible for him to receive a fair trial if he were charged. In England, he worked as a lawyer, wrote a textbook on law, and served as a queen's counsel.

Judas Iscariot was said to have betrayed Jesus to the Romans. The name is used to describe a person who would betray a friend.

A **counsel** is an attorney.

What is your opinion of a Jew playing an important role in the Confederate government?

A BLOW TO LIBERTY

In 1862, in the midst of the war, General Grant issued one of the most antisemitic orders in the history of the U.S. armed forces and, some would say, in U.S. history as a whole. General Order 11 expelled all Jews

Note-worthy

Judah Benjamin's picture is on the Confederate two-dollar bill.

from the border territory under his command, an area that included parts of Kentucky, Tennessee, and Mississippi. The order stated that the Jews were "as a class violating every regulation of trade established by the Treasury Department."

In general, the North prohibited trade with the South, viewing such activity as aiding the enemy. But there was a black market in Southern cotton. Both sides benefited: The North needed cotton for its factories, and the South needed war materiel, medical supplies, consumer goods, and gold and silver.

The **black market** is the illegal buying and selling of goods.

Materiel is the equipment, supplies, etc., used by an army or navy.

Lincoln had permitted some limited trade but insisted that it be licensed by the Treasury Department and the army. And in the territory under his control, Grant was in charge of issuing those licenses. Unlicensed traders, some of whom were Jews, tried to bribe Union officers to allow them to buy cotton without a permit. Although most of the illegal traders were not Jewish, in the heat of the war old prejudices reemerged.

Grant therefore became convinced that "mostly Jews and other unprincipled traders" had organized the black market. Although people from a variety of backgrounds were involved in the illegal trade, Jewish traders were singled out. Grant believed that the traders' activity was interrupting the movement of his troops, and at first he declared that "no Jews are to be permitted to travel on the railroad southward [into the Department of Tennessee] from any point" and that they were not to be given trade licenses. When the illegal trading continued, he issued Order 11.

The order was enforced immediately near Grant's headquarters in Mississippi, and some Jews had to walk forty miles to leave the area. In Paducah, Kentucky, the town's thirty Jewish families were given twenty-four hours to leave. The order was discussed widely in both the general and the Jewish press. In some cases, Grant was condemned; in others, Jews were blamed for criticizing Grant, a Union hero. Jews around the country gathered to protest. Many wrote to the president, urging him to annul the order.

General Order 11 December 17, 1862

The Jews, as a class violating every regulation of trade established by the Treasury Department and also department orders, are hereby expelled from the department within twenty-four hours from the receipt of this order.

Post commanders will see to it that all of this class of people be furnished passes and required to leave, and any one returning after such notification will be arrested and held in confinement until an opportunity occurs of sending them out as prisoners, unless furnished with permit from headquarters. No passes will be given these people to visit headquarters for the purpose of making personal application for trade permits.

By order of Maj. Gen. U.S. Grant

A group of Jewish businessmen from Paducah traveled to Washington to speak to Lincoln directly. Jewish leaders around the country organized protest rallies and sent telegrams to the White House. Jewish newspapers published editorials condemning the order. And two Jewish organizations, B'nai B'rith and the Board of Delegates of American Israelites, sent formal protests.

THINK ABOUT IT

Was what happened to the Jews of Paducah similar to or different from other expulsions in Jewish history? In what ways?

DO IT

Imagine that you live in Paducah and your family has just received word of Grant's Order 11. Describe your feelings in a letter to the president.

Cesar Kaskel was a Jewish businessman and community leader and the head of the group from Paducah that went to Washington to meet with Lincoln. Some stories have it that after studying the copies of the order that Kaskel had brought, Lincoln said, "And so the children of Israel were driven from the happy land of Canaan?" Kaskel is said to have answered, "Yes, and that is why we have come to Father Abraham's bosom seeking protection." And Lincoln reportedly replied, "And this protection they shall have."

President Lincoln instructed General Henry W. Halleck, a Union general, to have Grant's order withdrawn. Halleck complied, writing to Grant: "A paper **purporting** to be General Order No. 11, issued by you December 17, has been presented here. By its terms, it expels all Jews from your department. If such an order has been issued, it will be immediately revoked." Grant annulled the order three days later.

On January 6, Rabbi Wise led a delegation that met with Lincoln to thank him for his support. Expressing surprise that Grant had issued the order, the president declared that he would allow no American to be mistreated on the basis of religion. He said, "to condemn a class is, to say the least, to wrong the good with the bad." While General Order 11 was in effect, however, New York's *Jewish Record* reported that it was carried out efficiently. Jews were exiled from their homes, and their property was taken and destroyed. Jews whose sons were risking their lives for the Union cause felt betrayed.

Purporting means "claiming to be something."

What do you think President Lincoln meant when he said, "To condemn a class is, to say the least, to wrong the good with the bad"? Why were Jews singled out when other people were also involved in the black market?

THE "JEWISH VOTE"

The "Jewish vote" became an issue in the 1868 presidential campaign. The Democrats, in an effort to discredit the Republican candidate, Ulysses S. Grant, brought up General Order 11 as an example of Grant's

AMERICAN TELEGRAPH CO.,

Telegram on Halleck's order to revoke General Order No. 11.

supposed antisemitism. Grant initially refused to apologize for the incident, and Jews were divided in their response. Should they decide that a voter's religion was separate from his politics, or should they vote as Jews?

Isaac Mayer Wise, a longtime Democrat, urged Jews to vote against Grant because of his antisemitism. Wise could not understand how Jews could separate their Judaism from the rest of their lives. He said, "We have been trying quite seriously to make of our humble self two Isaac M. Wises. The one who is a citizen of the State of Ohio, and the other who is a Jew, but we failed and we failed decidedly."

Others disagreed, either fearing the consequences of mixing politics and religion or wanting to forgive Grant because of the difficult situation facing him during the war. Grant finally answered the many letters he received and the articles in the press with a statement in response to a letter from a man named Adolph Moses. He said:

"I do not pretend to sustain the order. At the time of its publication, I was incensed by a reprimand received from Washington for permitting acts which Jews within my lines were engaged in. . . . The order was issued and sent without any reflection and without thinking of the Jews as a sect or race to themselves, but simply as persons who had successfully . . . violated an order. . . . Give Mr. Moses assurance that I have no prejudice against sect or race, but want each individual to be judged by his own merit." It seemed, in the end that many Jews voted according to their party loyalties rather than their interests as Jews.

After he became president, Grant displayed significant concern for Jewish interests and appointed a number of Jews to important diplomatic and other government posts. He refused to discuss General Order 11 and did not write about it in his memoirs, apparently wishing to let the controversy die.

THE WAR'S END

As Jews prepared to celebrate Passover in 1865, the nation's bloodiest war ended on April 9 with the surrender of the Confederate States of America's General Robert E. Lee to General Ulysses S. Grant at Appomattox Courthouse, Virginia. Throughout the North, Jews gave thanks for their ancestors' freedom from slavery in Egypt and for the end of the war.

Less than a week later, however, on April 14, on the eve of the fifth day of Passover, the actor John Wilkes Booth assassinated President Lincoln. Jews joined in the national mourning for the fallen president. Synagogues filled, black drapes were hung, Yom Kippur hymns were substituted for Passover songs, and rabbis spoke of their deep grief.

Lincoln's body went by train from city to city so that Americans could pay their respects to the fallen president. Jews were among the members of special committees that escorted the train. On a canopy over the coffin were the words that King David had said about Saul: "Precious Israel, upon your heights lie the slain" (Samuel 21:19).

The largest demonstration was held in New York City, where thousands of Jews marched in the funeral pageant, Jewish leaders sat with the official dignitaries, and Reverend Samuel M. Isaacs was one of the religious leaders who spoke.

THINK ABOUT IT

Why was it important for Jews to be equally represented with other citizens in mourning President Lincoln? Why were they so committed to doing so?

THE WAR'S AFTERMATH

During the Civil War, Southerners had serious concerns about their survival. Because the white male population of the South was smaller than that of the North, more Southern families found themselves without men to share the work and head households. The burden was especially heavy in families that owned no slaves and lacked the means to feed themselves. Many women and blacks entered the workforce. As they did, wages declined sharply.

Most Southerners suffered from the lack of food, manufactured goods, and medicine. The South had traditionally depended on imported manufactured goods, but with Union troops blockading many Southern ports, most shipments never reached their destination. Food supplies were limited because the Union army often used Southern crops to feed themselves, or simply destroyed them. By 1864 in Richmond, a dozen eggs cost six dollars and a pound of butter cost twenty-five dollars. Instead of growing cash crops, such as cotton and tobacco, many Southerners were forced to grow their own food.

Toward the end of the war, the Union army followed a strategy of destroying Southern civilians' means of supporting themselves. This plan of wrecking plantations and farms successfully weakened the Confederacy. As Union troops advanced, many Southerners fled their homes and suddenly found themselves homeless and without land on which to grow crops. Others stayed, living alongside the Union soldiers who often destroyed their homes and terrorized them. By December 1864, the desertion rate in the Confederate army was more than 50 percent. Some men wanted to return to their families; others just wanted to be finished with the bloody war.

DO IT

Imagine your seder in 1865, just after hearing that the Civil War is over. Choose one of the traditional Passover symbols to create a ritual to celebrate the end of the war.

After the war, the South was in ruins. And although Lincoln's Emancipation Proclamation, issued January 1, 1863, had freed slaves in areas still under Confederate control, that freedom did not become a reality until after the war ended. The new president, Andrew Johnson, faced an awesome task.

THINK ABOUT IT

What do you think of the intentional destruction of civilian property in a war? Look at Deuteronomy 20:19 to see what Judaism says about unnecessary destruction of property. What are your thoughts?

In the South, synagogues—as well as so much else—had been destroyed. And like other Southerners, Jews had to make sense of the fact that so many men had fought and died for a cause that had been defeated. Many Southern Jews set aside special sections of their cemeteries for members of their communities who had been killed in the war. They observed Confederate Memorial Day and built monuments to the Jewish war dead in many of their cemeteries. Moses Ezekiel, a Jewish sculptor, created the *New South* monument to Confederate soldiers at Arlington National Cemetery, as well as a monument called *Virginia Mourning Her Dead.*

In the North, Jews celebrated the end of slavery and the preservation of the Union. Northerners did not suffer the same deprivations as Southerners did, and the postwar economic boom brought new prosperity to much of the country, including many Jewish communities. The demand for uniforms during the war expanded the ready-made clothing industry in which many Jews made their fortunes. When the war ended, newly arrived Jewish tailors from Europe helped the American industry to produce fashionable clothes at affordable prices.

LEARN IT

Deprivation means "scarcity, lack."

Prosperity means "wealth."

As Jews grew wealthier, they built flourishing religious and communal institutions in many cities. The Jewish communities in Cincinnati, New York, San Francisco, and Philadelphia grew and expanded their synagogues. In Cincinnati, Rabbi Isaac Mayer Wise's Congregation Bene Yeshurun, the second largest congregation in America, built the Plum Street Temple, which was dedicated in 1866. It was prominently located across from the city hall and the city's main Catholic and Unitarian churches, and its architecture clearly announced to the world that the building was a synagogue. In colonial times, some synagogues in America, such as the Touro Synagogue in Newport, Rhode Island, did not look like synagogues from the outside. Now, however, Jews were proud to be identified as Jews. And by calling itself a "temple," and having an organ, choir loft, and pews where men and women sat together, this synagogue was also demonstrating its congregation's affiliation with the growing Reform movement.

THINK ABOUT IT

What message did the Civil War and its aftermath send to American Jews about their country?

Crossword puzzle

Solve the crossword puzzle using the last names of persons you read about in Chapters 1–3.

ACROSS

2. Jewish commander at Gettysburg
5. Winner of the Congressional Medal of Honor
6. Staunch American Jewish supporter of women's rights
7. Author of "The Bible View of Slavery"
9. The encyclopedist and scholar who rejected the "Bible View" of Slavery
10. Rabbi and supporter of secession
12. The "brains" of the Confederacy

DOWN

1. Rabbi, author of patriotic sermons, and critic of "The Bible View of Slavery" who ran for his life
2. Jewish resident of Talbotton
3. Confederate envoy to Europe
4. Galveston spy
5. Jewish resident of Paducah who protested General Order 11
8. Inmate of Ship Island
11. Rabbi, Democrat, and critic of Grant

Ask your teacher to check your answers in the Teaching Guide.

The historic Plum Street Temple in Cincinnati, Ohio

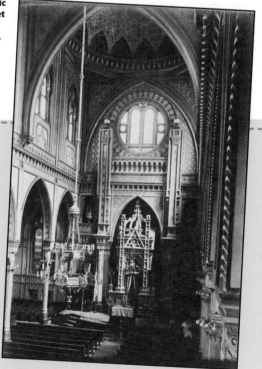

Growing Numbers

In 1860, there were seventy-seven synagogues in the United States accommodating 34,412 worshippers. By 1870, there were 152 synagogues serving 73,265 worshippers. By 1880, there were between 240,000 and 250,000 Jews in the United States. In 1890 there were 533 synagogues and in the next thirty years these numbers would increase dramatically as Jews emigrated from Eastern Europe.

UNIT 1 TIME LINE OF HISTORICAL EVENTS: THE CIVIL WAR AND THE JEWS

| | 1830 | 1832 | 1834 | 1836 | 1838 | 1840 | 1842 | 1844 | 1846 | 1848 | 185 |

AMERICA

1831: The first horse-drawn buses appear in New York; Nat Turner leads a slave revolt in Virginia.

1834: Abraham Lincoln enters politics as an assemblyman in the Illinois legislature; Walter Hunt of New York constructs one of the first sewing machines.

1837: The U.S. Congress passes the Gag Law to stop debate on slavery.

1839: Abner Doubleday lays out the first baseball field and conducts the first game.

1843: Congress gives Morse $30,000 to build the first telegraph line from Washington to Baltimore.

1846: Iowa becomes a state; Smithsonian Institution in Washington, D.C., is founded.

1849: High Holiday services are held in a tent in San Francisco.

JEWISH AMERICA

1838: Isaac Leeser publishes the first Hebrew primer for children in U.S.; Rebecca Gratz starts Hebrew Sunday School in Philadelphia.

1840: Abraham Rice, America's first ordained rabbi, immigrates to America and takes a pulpit in Baltimore.

1845: Isaac Leeser publishes an English translation of the Torah.

JEWISH WORLD

1831: Jews in Jamaica get the right to vote after living there since 1655; France provides public support for synagogues.

1832: Canada grants Jews political rights; Benedict Stilling of Germany proposes that retina transplants can cure some blindness.

1833: Jews are admitted to the Bar to practice law in England.

1837: An earthquake in Safed and Tiberius kills thousands and damages archeological sites.

1839: The Sultan of Turkey issues a Bill of Rights for all non-Muslims; a clothes tax is put on Jews in Lithuania (wearing a kipah costs 5 rubles a year).

1840: Jews are falsely accused of murdering a Capuchin monk in the "Damascus Affair;" The Jewish community in India establishes the first Hebrew printing press there.

1847: Lionel Rothschild, the first Jew elected to England's House of Commons, refuses to take a Christian oath and is not allowed to take his seat.

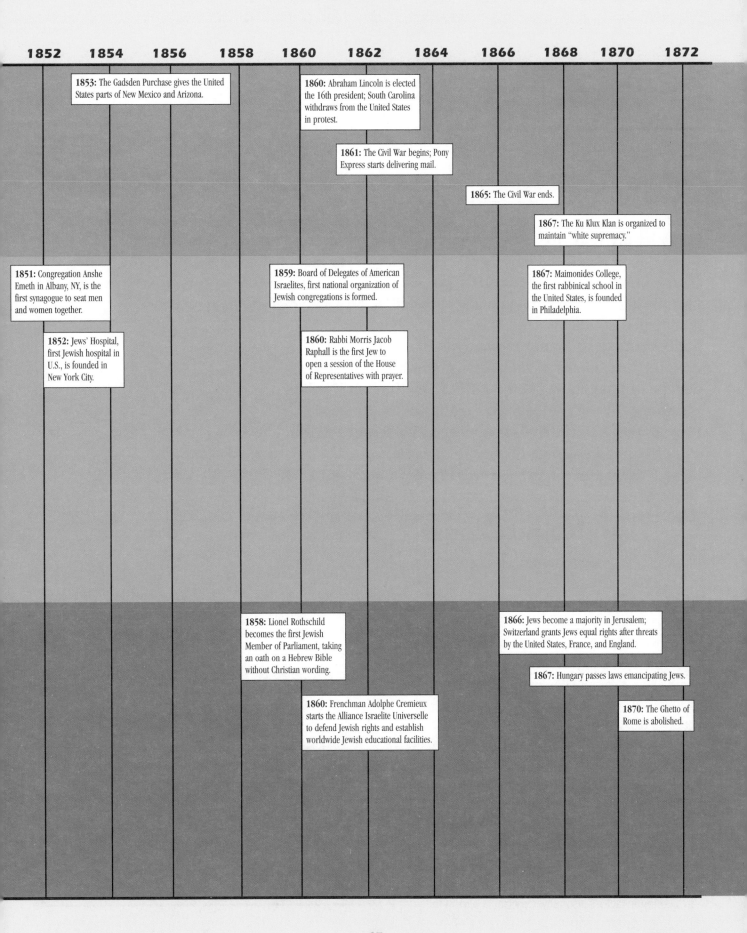

1853: The Gadsden Purchase gives the United States parts of New Mexico and Arizona.

1860: Abraham Lincoln is elected the 16th president; South Carolina withdraws from the United States in protest.

1861: The Civil War begins; Pony Express starts delivering mail.

1865: The Civil War ends.

1867: The Ku Klux Klan is organized to maintain "white supremacy."

1851: Congregation Anshe Emeth in Albany, NY, is the first synagogue to seat men and women together.

1859: Board of Delegates of American Israelites, first national organization of Jewish congregations is formed.

1867: Maimonides College, the first rabbinical school in the United States, is founded in Philadelphia.

1852: Jews' Hospital, first Jewish hospital in U.S., is founded in New York City.

1860: Rabbi Morris Jacob Raphall is the first Jew to open a session of the House of Representatives with prayer.

1858: Lionel Rothschild becomes the first Jewish Member of Parliament, taking an oath on a Hebrew Bible without Christian wording.

1866: Jews become a majority in Jerusalem; Switzerland grants Jews equal rights after threats by the United States, France, and England.

1867: Hungary passes laws emancipating Jews.

1860: Frenchman Adolphe Cremieux starts the Alliance Israelite Universelle to defend Jewish rights and establish worldwide Jewish educational facilities.

1870: The Ghetto of Rome is abolished.

CHAPTER 4
COMING TO AMERICA

Who were the Jews of the Great Migration, and why did they come to the United States?

"**G**ive me your tired, your poor, your huddled masses yearning to breathe free . . . Send these, the homeless, tempest-tossed, to me, I lift my lamp beside the golden door." These words, inscribed on the base of the Statue of Liberty, express the promise of America. The promise, penned by an American Jew named Emma Lazarus, has been the hope of immigrants to this country since its founding. It was certainly the dream of the massive number of Eastern European Jews, more than 2 million of whom arrived on the shores of the United States from Russia, Romania, Poland, and Austria-Hungary between 1880 and 1924, in what became known as the Great Migration.

A **tempest** is a storm.

Emma Lazarus's original manuscript for 'The New Colossus.'

WHY DID THEY COME?

By 1880, the population of the United States was just over 50 million, and the Jewish population was 250,000. Between 1880 and 1920, some 23 million immigrants entered the country. The vast majority of them came from European nations, especially Italy and Russia. Approximately 2 million of those immigrants were Jews. Whereas most of the Jews living in the United States in 1880 had come from Central Europe, most of the new Jewish immigrants came from Eastern Europe.

Changes that had begun in Eastern Europe in the 1860s prompted many people to abandon their homes and make their way to America. For example, a nationalist movement in Poland failed in 1863. Poles had been trying to regain their independence since Russia occupied the country in the late 1700s; now they were bitterly disappointed. In Lithuania in 1867–1868, a famine worsened conditions among the Jews, as did a cholera epidemic in Poland in 1869.

Economic factors also played a critical part in the migration. As a result of industrialization, many merchants, peddlers, artisans, and innkeepers lost their jobs. At the same time, the Jewish population in all of Europe quadrupled, resulting in greater competition and poverty. In Russia, the serfs were liberated by Czar Alexander II in 1861. Newly free, they were often in debt and unable to trade with or pay the local merchants, most of whom were Jewish. All of those factors contributed to terrible poverty in the Jewish community.

A **nationalist movement** is the coming together of regions of a country or groups of people to form a unified whole. It involves the development of an identity among people who have some common history, language, customs, and beliefs.

A **serf** is a person who works on a landowner's property and can be transferred with that property to a new landowner.

Emma Lazarus and "The New Colossus"

Emma Lazarus, a well-known American Jewish poet and writer in the nineteenth century, is best remembered for "The New Colossus." In 1883, the Pedestal Art Loan Exhibition was held to raise funds for the building of the Statue of Liberty's pedestal. The statue was a gift from the people of France to the people of the United States, but funds for the statue's base had to be raised privately in the United States. Famous writers, including Walt Whitman and Mark Twain, contributed original manuscripts for the Pedestal Art Loan Exhibition's auction. A friend of Lazarus's who was involved in the event asked her to write a poem for it. Lazarus replied that she couldn't "write to order." Knowing that she had been working as a volunteer with Jewish immigrants at a settlement house on New York's Lower East Side, the friend suggested that Lazarus find her inspiration in her settlement house work. A few days later, Lazarus sent her friend the poem.

Not like the brazen giant of Greek fame,
With conquering limbs astride from land to land;
Here at our sea-washed, sunset gates shall stand
A mighty woman with a torch, whose flame
Is the imprisoned lightning, and her name
Mother of Exiles. From her beacon-hand
Glows world-wide welcome;
her mild eyes command
The air-bridged harbor that twin cities frame.
"Keep, ancient lands,
your storied pomp!" cries she
With silent lips. "Give me your tired, your poor,
Your huddled masses yearning to breathe free,
The wretched refuse of your teeming shore,
Send these, the homeless, tempest-tossed to me,
I lift my lamp beside the golden door!"

LOOK AT IT

Years later when the poem was about to be inscribed on the base of the Statue of Liberty, a banker named Samuel Ward Gray objected to the terms "huddled masses" and "wretched refuse." His suggestion, which was not accepted, was to change the eleventh and twelfth lines to "Your stirring myriad, that yearn to breathe free, But find no place upon your teeming shore."

 LEARN IT

A **colossus** is a statue or image of the human form of very large dimensions.

Brazen means "bold."

Pomp is a stately, splendid, and perhaps indulgent display.

Refuse is something that is discarded as worthless or useless.

Teeming means "crowded."

Myriad means "many."

DO IT

Write a poem here or draw a picture on a separate sheet that you would like to see engraved on the pedestal of the Statue of Liberty.

_____
_____
_____
_____
_____
_____

THINK ABOUT IT

What do you think of the terms that offended Gray? What did they reflect about people's attitudes toward immigrants at that time? Do some Americans hold similar attitudes today? What is your opinion of Gray's suggested changes?

Beginning in 1855, when he became czar of Russia, Alexander II had initiated reforms that had improved the lives of many Russians, including the country's Jews. He had also repealed some anti-Jewish measures and allowed certain Jews to settle in the country's interior. In 1881, after a revolutionary assassinated him, the situation of Russia's Jews deteriorated rapidly. Rumors spread regarding Jewish involvement in the assassination, and Alexander III ended his father's reforms and renewed suppression of the Jews, beginning with a wave of pogroms in 1881. Pogroms arose in 225 cities and towns in 1881 and 1882, destroying some 20,000 Jewish homes and leaving tens of thousands of Jews economically ruined. Alexander III justified the pogroms as legitimate expressions of peasant anger against their Jewish "oppressors." (Other major waves of pogroms would follow in 1903–1906 and 1917–1920, each more violent than the previous one. All of them had an important impact on Jewish emigration from Eastern Europe; immigration rates rose sharply after each incident.) In May 1882, Alexander III enacted the "temporary laws" or "May laws," which renewed persecution of the empire's Jews.

The Jews of the Russian Empire had been largely restricted to the so-called Pale of Settlement, the territory where Jews were legally permitted to reside. This included, by the end of the nineteenth century, Russia's western-most provinces, as well as the old Kingdom of Poland, incorporated into Russia in 1815. For more than two hundred years, most Russian Jews had been confined to small towns known in Yiddish as *shtetlach* (the plural of *shtetl*). Laws had isolated them and restricted certain privileges, such as owning land. Now, the May laws reduced the size of the Pale by 10 percent and limited the number of Jews permitted to attend secondary schools and universities. They forbade Jews to settle in villages (forcing 500,000 from rural areas), own or rent property outside of towns, become lawyers, hold civil service jobs, or conduct business on Sundays or Christian holidays. By 1891, an additional 700,000 Jews had been expelled from other parts of Russia and forced to move into the Pale. The "temporary laws" remained in effect until 1917, when Czar Nicholas II was overthrown at the start of the Russian Revolution.

How might you have reacted to the "temporary laws" had you lived in Eastern Europe at the time?

Suppression refers to the act of holding or putting people down by force.

A **pogrom** is an organized riot directed at a group of people with the intention of burning and looting their property and injuring or killing them. Specifically it refers to actions carried out against the Jews in Russia or Russian-controlled Poland.

A **pale** is a territory or district within certain bounds or under a particular jurisdiction.

The first May law

"As a temporary measure, and until a general revision is made of their legal status, it is decreed that the Jews be forbidden to settle anew outside of towns and boroughs, exceptions being admitted only in the case of existing Jewish agricultural colonies."

The Kishinev pogrom, 1903

On Easter morning 1903, the quiet in the city of Kishinev was broken by a storm of violence when a group of youths assaulted some Jews and broke windows. A few hours later, small groups of men entered the Jewish section of the city, cursing, looting, destroying property, and attacking anyone who opposed them. The Russian government had fostered anti-Jewish propaganda, and the police now stood on the sidelines, acting only to accept a share of the stolen items. By the next day, others, now armed with clubs and axes, had joined the riot. The police arrested those Jews who tried to defend themselves. Later in the day, after receiving orders from the government, the police moved in and cleared the streets without firing a shot. About fifty Jews were killed, more than 500 were injured, 600 shops were destroyed, and 700 homes were ruined.

An American response: The American Jewish Committee

A group of German-American Jews led by financier Jacob Schiff, Philadelphia judge Mayor Sulzberger, and attorney Louis Marshall wished to respond to the pogroms in Kishinev. They gathered in New York City on November 11, 1906, to create the American Jewish Committee. Their goal was to "protect Jewish rights wherever they are threatened."

Visit the AJC website at www.ajc.org to learn what this organization does today.

A DIFFICULT DECISION

These worsening political, economic, and social conditions motivated large numbers of Eastern European Jews to emigrate. Lower steamship rates, steamship-company promotions, letters from relatives who had already settled abroad, and the widely publicized image of America as a land of opportunity, the *goldene medinah,* or "golden land," as it was known in Yiddish, persuaded many immigrants to set sail for the United States. Although they were fleeing poverty and discrimination in their homeland, such a trip was a major decision for people who had rarely traveled far from their villages. With only a few exceptions, the first Jews who emigrated, between 1870 and 1900, usually had little to lose in terms of status and wealth.

Palestine was another destination, especially for the early Zionists. After the 1881–1882 pogroms, many Eastern European Jews came to believe that it was their responsibility to build a Jewish homeland. Nonetheless, most Eastern European Jews believed that America was their land of opportunity. Some 80 percent of all Jews leaving Russia came to the United States, while only about 3 percent went to the Holy Land. Significant numbers went to other countries as well, including Canada, Australia, Argentina, South Africa and countries in western Europe.

Would you have chosen to go to Palestine, the United States, or some other country? Why?

Many Jews remained in Russia because they did not want to leave the life they had established or because they hoped to build a better society there. Some Jews would not even consider going to America because they saw it as a *treife medinah*, a place where they could not live a religious Jewish life. In fact, some of Eastern Europe's leading Orthodox rabbis opposed immigration to the United States. Without the strict rabbinic authority that they provided, the rabbis feared that Jews would fall away from Judaism.

Rabbi Israel Meir ha-Kohen, who was known by the name of his most popular book, the *Hafetz Hayim (Seeker of Life)*, advised immigrants not to settle in countries like America. "If because of hard circumstances" one is "compelled to journey there," he wrote, ". . . let him return home [as soon as possible] and trust to the Lord who provides for all." He also warned against remaining "for the sake of riches in a land many of whose inhabitants have broken away from religion." Other rabbis, such as Pinhas Michael, of Antopol, a *shtetl* in Belarus, recommended: "travel to America; there you will make a living." He felt it necessary to add, however: "Preserve the Sabbath."

Wearing a tallit and tefillin during morning prayers

The rabbis' fears were not unfounded. One rabbi who immigrated to America in 1885 reported that many of his fellow passengers on the voyage ate nonkosher food. Another rabbi said that even aboard ship many of the Jewish immigrants had already stopped reciting daily prayers and using their *tallitot* and *tefillin*. Yet another rabbi later recalled that when dining at the Hebrew Immigrant Aid Society's kosher dining room at Ellis Island, some immigrants failed to perform the ritual washing of their hands and recited neither the Motzi, nor the Birkat Hamazon.

Treife is the feminine form of *treif*, food that is not kosher.

Tallitot is the plural of *tallit*, a prayer shawl.

Tefillin are small boxes containing the four biblical passages (Exodus 13:1–10, Exodus 13:11–16, Deuteronomy 6:4–9, and Deuteronomy 11:13–21) in which it is commanded that the verse be bound to a worshipper's left arm and forehead. Black leather straps attached to the boxes enable them to be worn, and they are traditionally donned during the weekday morning prayer service.

The **Motzi** is the blessing recited before eating bread; it is said before meals.

The **Birkat Hamazon** is the prayer recited after a meal.

What do you think of the rabbis' opposition to immigration? How would you make a decision that balances your religious life as a Jew against your need for physical safety and a way of earning a living? Picture yourself having a discussion with your rabbi. What would you say?

Among some immigrant groups, men came alone, planning to make money and return home. Many Jewish immigrants, however, came with their families; the numbers of men and women were roughly equal and one out of every four was a child below the age of fourteen. They were fleeing poverty and discrimination in their homeland and such a trip was a major undertaking, so few chose to return. In fact, some who had returned to Europe earlier came back to the United States as conditions in Europe worsened. Often, however, whole families could not afford to emigrate together, so the men came first and lived frugally until they could raise enough money to bring the rest of the family.

One family's story

Beryl Kapnek was likely born in 1851, probably in Berdichev, near Kiev, in Russia. It is impossible to be certain because all the public records from 1850 to 1900 for that area have been lost. Moreover, pre-1850 archives include a number of Kapneks in the town. Berdichev was the center of the publishing business in the Ukraine, and more than half the population of about 120,000 residents were Jewish. Beryl's wife, Deborah, was born in 1852 in the same area.

Beryl Kapnek and Deborah Behrman were married in 1872 and eventually had nine children. Beryl was a coppersmith and worked on the copper domes of Russian Orthodox churches. When the priests declared that Jews would no longer be permitted to work on the churches, the couple began planning to take their family to America.

In 1889, Beryl Kapnek and his two oldest sons, Samuel, age ten, and James, age eight, left for America, leaving Deborah behind with their five daughters, Brucha (Rebecca), age fifteen; Molly, twelve; Sara, seven; Irene, five; and Rose, three; and their newborn son, William. For the next nine years, Beryl and his sons lived in Philadelphia and saved their money in order to bring Deborah and the other children to America. Since Beryl could not find work as a coppersmith, he went to work in a factory that made steamer trunks and metal suitcases.

During those nine years, the oldest daughter, Rebecca, married and came to America with her husband and two-year-old daughter. Just as their ship was arriving, in 1895, a second daughter was born. Two years later, Beryl was finally able to send for his wife and children. Their ninth and last child, Edith, was born in Philadelphia in 1898. (Historical information compiled by Louis Glickman of Sarasota, Florida.)

THINK ABOUT IT Think about how difficult it must have been to be separated from members of your family for nine years. How might you have felt when you were reunited?

DO IT Imagine that you are Samuel Kapnek, and write a letter to your mother and siblings in Russia. Or imagine that you are Brucha Kapnek, and write a letter to your father and brothers in America. Describe what is happening to you in the Old Country or in the New World, and tell how you feel about it.

_____
_____
_____
_____
_____
_____
_____
_____
_____
_____
_____
_____
_____
_____
_____
_____

Some single men and women chose to come alone, even against their parents' wishes, leaving behind family and friends in order to avoid the military draft, escape poverty, and seek a new life in America. Traveling alone was particularly difficult for women; they were questioned closely and sometimes held at the immigration centers until family members arrived to escort them to their new homes. Some Jewish organizations, especially the National Council of Jewish Women, developed programs to assist single women.

 Imagine that you are living in the Pale and your parents tell you that they have decided to immigrate to America. What might you hope and dream? What might you fear? Now imagine that you are in your twenties, old enough to travel alone. Would you emigrate? Why or why not?

A DIFFICULT JOURNEY

Despite the difficulty of making the decision to emigrate, approximately one-third of Eastern European Jews ultimately chose to leave their homeland. They had to scrape together the money, often relying on funds sent to them by family members who had already reached America. Although shipping costs declined during this time, providing another motivation for emigration, many families raised the money to pay for passports, transportation to a port city, passage on a ship, food and shelter along the way, and landing fees only by selling most of their possessions. Acquiring a passport frequently required a three-month wait, although those able to pay the local officials who set the prices could get one faster. Young men who were eligible for the army often had to be smuggled out of the country. Because they had no passport or identification papers, it was often necessary to bribe government officials along the way. The cost of a ticket on a ship, even in steerage, was expensive: It might cost twenty-five dollars from Liverpool, England, (about $420 in 1997 terms), and thirty-four dollars from Hamburg, Germany, or Antwerp, Belgium (about $570 in 1997 terms). Thus, people reached the United States with few possessions and whatever skills they had learned.

 Steerage is the lowest class of accommodation on a passenger ship.

The journey by ship took between thirteen and twenty days, depending on the time of year. Most immigrants traveled in steerage, which was overcrowded and had only primitive sanitary facilities. A few basins served as dishpans, laundry tubs, and sinks, and toilets were open troughs that were rarely cleaned. Some shipping companies locked their steerage compartments so that passengers could not go onto the upper decks and associate with passengers traveling in second class. In the early days, the food was not kosher and was so dreadful that even those who were not observant often could not eat it. The immigrants persevered only for the promise of a new life in America. They knew that there was no czar in America, and agents for the steamship companies had lured many of them with stories of a wonderful land where they could quickly and easily make their fortune. One man said, "In our minds, we were coming to a country of wonders and mystery. I had imagined that all Americans were tall and slender and that all men wore yellow trousers and high hats."

THE IMMIGRANTS ARRIVE

Crowded processing centers awaited those who reached America at the ports of New York, Philadelphia, Boston, and Baltimore. Immigrants immediately received physical examinations, and symbols were drawn with chalk on the coats of those with medical problems. Immigration officials often commented on the poor physical state of the immigrants. Between 1887 and 1890, about 5,000 Jewish immigrants were sent back to Europe because the officials thought them "unfit for work." Yet although Jewish immigrants suffered from tuberculosis and other ailments, their health was remarkably good, especially when compared with that of other immigrants.

The busiest port was New York City, first at Castle Garden and later at Ellis Island. At times, as many as 4,000 immigrants arrived each day. For Jewish immigrants the process included an interview by a representative of a Jewish charity, who was sometimes less sympathetic to their condition than were the government officials. Despite the

A story by Sholem Aleichem

The most important Jewish writer to come to America during this period was Sholem Rabinovich, better known as Sholem Aleichem. He first came in 1906, but disliked the country so much that he returned to Russia after only a few months. When the First World War began, he came to America again. In a story called "Off for the Golden Land," this famous Yiddish author wrote about the medical examination that the immigrants endured:

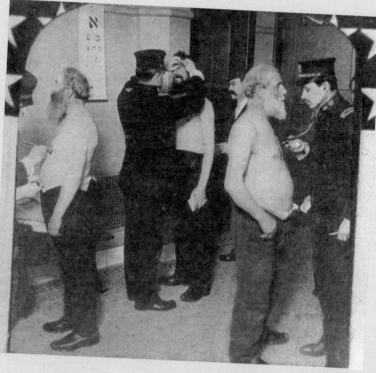

The time comes to go on board the ship. People tell them that they should take a walk to the doctor. So they go to the doctor. The doctor examines them and finds they are all hale and hearty and can go to America, but she, that is Goldele, cannot go, because she has trachomas *on her eyes. At first her family did not understand. Only later did they realize it. That meant that they could all go to America but she, Goldele, would have to remain here in Antwerp. So there began a wailing, a weeping, a moaning. Three times her mamma fainted. Her papa wanted to stay here, but he couldn't. All the ship tickets would be lost. So they had to go off to America and leave her, Goldele, here until the trachomas would go away from her eyes.*

Trachoma is a contagious inflammation of the eye.

from Deborah Dwork, "Immigrant Jews on the Lower East Side of New York, 1880–1914," in *The American Jewish Experience* **ed. Jonathan D. Sarna, (New York: Holmes and Meier, 1997)**

aid offered them, many immigrants thought the experience was harsh. In her autobiography, *Living My Life*, Emma Goldman wrote: "The atmosphere [was] charged with antagonism and harshness. Nowhere could one see a sympathetic face; there was no provision for comfort of the new arrivals. . . . The first day on American soil proved a violent shock." Abraham Cahan, editor and founder of the Yiddish paper, *The Forverts*, wrote of his arrival at Castle Garden: "My heart grew even heavier when they began to register us. I felt we were being treated like recruits at a Russian summons for military service."

THINK ABOUT IT Why might some Jews already living in America have been antagonistic to the Jewish immigrants?

Although at first some leaders of the existing Jewish organizations did not understand the new immigrants' needs, other Jewish groups soon volunteered to help. A network of organizations became involved with processing the Jewish immigrants at the docks, finding housing and employment for them, and performing other social services. A group calling itself the Hebrew Immigrant Aid Society (HIAS) was formed to provide meals and transportation for the new immigrants.

HIAS representatives worked on Ellis Island, making immediate help available to the arriving Jews. They offered translation services, assisted with medical screening and other procedures, lent some immigrants the twenty-five dollar landing fee, and tried to persuade officials not to deport some of the immigrants. They located relatives for many immigrants who could not find family members to help them get started in America.

In 1909, HIAS merged with the Hebrew Sheltering House Association, and in 1911 it had a kosher kitchen installed on Ellis Island. It also provided religious services and musical concerts, ran an employment bureau, and sold railroad tickets at reduced fares to immigrants who were leaving New York for other cities.

If you cannot visit New York, visit one of the excellent Ellis Island websites. Try the American Family Immigration History Center at www.ellisisland.org for stories of people who have researched their ancestors (including a story by a Jewish man), and a searchable database. Another website is the Ellis Island Immigration Museum at www.ellisisland.com. Click on "History" and "Timeline" to view its time line. The History Channel, at www.historychannel.com/ellisisland, includes photographs and activities for building a family tree and determining whether you would have been allowed into the United States. Finally, the government's www.nps.gov/ellis provides a history and photographs of Ellis Island.

Visit the HIAS website at www.hias.org. What does HIAS do today?

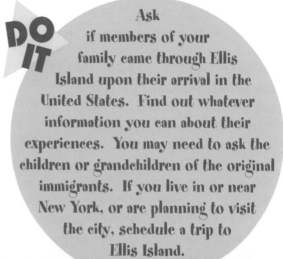

Ask if members of your family came through Ellis Island upon their arrival in the United States. Find out whatever information you can about their experiences. You may need to ask the children or grandchildren of the original immigrants. If you live in or near New York, or are planning to visit the city, schedule a trip to Ellis Island.

SEPHARDIC JEWS

Not all Jews who immigrated to the United States between 1880 and 1920 came from Eastern Europe. Other Jews left communities in Turkey, Greece, Syria, and the Balkan countries, as well as parts of Asia and northeast Africa, lands that had been ruled by Muslim Turks for centuries. Toward the end of the nineteenth century, a social and intellectual revolution was taking place in many of these Sephardic communities. After centuries of isolation, modern ideas were reaching the people. Much of this change was brought about by schools run by the Alliance Israelite Universelle, a Paris-based Jewish organization that aimed to bring modern French education to children living in the Ottoman Empire. This education created a desire to seek a better life, and the idea of immigrating to America caught on.

At first, this immigration movement was small. Soon, however, conditions in Turkey and the Balkan countries, provided Jews with the impetus to leave. A revolution in Turkey in 1908, aimed at instituting a constitutional government, created hardships for many Jews. Compulsory military service was instituted, and Jews were included in the draft for the first time. Turkey was involved in a war with Italy in 1911–1912, and fires and earthquakes damaged many cities. Life was very difficult, and many people were poverty-stricken. During the Balkan Wars of 1912–1913, there was a great deal of violence, and many Jewish communities were destroyed. In contrast to these terrible conditions, life in America seemed even more appealing.

The 20,000 Sephardic Jews who came to the United States between 1900 and 1920 settled mostly on the Lower East Side of New York, in their own small communities. They spoke Judeo-Spanish, now known as Ladino, and many of the Yiddish-speaking Jews thought they were Italian or members of some other Mediterranean group and failed to identify them as Jews. At first, therefore, they received almost no aid from the Jewish organizations that assisted other Jewish immigrants. Moise Gadol, who had emigrated from Bulgaria, approached the leaders of HIAS and in 1911 persuaded them to establish the Oriental Bureau dedicated to serving the needs of the Sephardic immigrants.

Gadol, who also edited a weekly Judeo-Spanish newspaper, *La America,* was the only employee of the Oriental Bureau. He helped the Sephardic immigrants complete citizenship papers and find jobs. The immigrants started restaurants and established synagogues, burial societies, and a benevolent society that became the Sephardic Brotherhood of America. In 1912, the Federation of Oriental Jews was established, and the Sisterhood of Congregation Shearith Israel, the oldest Spanish-Portuguese synagogue in New York, established a settlement house on the Lower East Side to assist them. [from Marc D. Angel, *La America: The Sephardic Experience in the United States* (Philadelphia, PA: Jewish Publication Society, 1982)]

Balkan countries are the nations on the Balkan Peninsula in southeast Europe. In the context of the Balkan wars against the Ottoman Empire, these were Serbia, Bulgaria, Greece, and Montenegro. A current definition would also include Albania, Bosnia, Herzegovina, Croatia, Macedonia, Romania, Slovenia, and Turkey.

Impetus means "momentum" or "drive."

Judeo-Spanish/Ladino and **Yiddish** are Jewish dialects that combine Hebrew with the languages of the local people: Spanish for Ladino and German for Yiddish.

A **federation** is a centrally governed group made up of several smaller groups.

BUT THEY MADE IT

Despite the obstacles, an enormous number of Jewish immigrants landed on U.S. shores before Congress passed a law in 1921 limiting the number of immigrants to 300,000 per year. The Johnson-Reed Immigration Act of 1924 limited immigration even more sharply. Yet those who arrived during the Great Migration were to change the face of the American Jewish community forever.

Galveston, oh, Galveston

While most Jewish immigrants entered the United States through New York, there was a little-known and not very successful project that brought Jewish immigrants to Texas. Some American Jewish leaders believed that settling immigrants in the Midwest and the Southwest would help alleviate crowding in the larger cities and would therefore reduce the likelihood of antisemitism. Thus, the Galveston immigration movement was initiated in 1907.

Galveston, Texas, was chosen for several reasons. Lloyds Shipping Company, which served the German port of Bremen, a point of departure for many Eastern European Jews, already stopped at Galveston, and railroads connected it to major cities in the Southwest and Midwest. In addition, Rabbi Henry Cohen, considered one of the most prominent Jewish leaders of the time, was the rabbi of the Galveston community, and he met almost every ship carrying Jewish immigrants and helped direct them to new homes.

Immigrants about to enter the United States through Galveston, Texas.

Jacob Schiff, the New York banker and philanthropist, developed the plan and donated $500,000 to put it into practice. He sought help from Israel Zangwill, the director of the Jewish Territorial Organization in Europe, asking that he supply the immigrants. Morris Waldman, the first manager of the Jewish Immigrants' Information Bureau connected with the Industrial Removal Office, traveled around the South and the West, identifying communities that would provide jobs and housing for the immigrants. When immigrants arrived in Galveston, Waldman gave them train tickets and the information he had gathered about jobs and housing in other cities.

The stay in Galveston was brief—only twelve to twenty-four hours. Immigrants soon boarded trains heading for their new homes. They mainly settled between the Mississippi River and the Rocky Mountains; few remained in Galveston. The project sought healthy laborers and skilled workers under the age of forty. The number of Hebrew teachers and kosher butchers was restricted because it was thought that their traditional religious observance would hinder their ability to find work and assimilate.

The program, which lasted until 1914, brought only about 10,000 immigrants through Galveston. It collapsed for several reasons: the struggling U.S. economy, increasingly restrictive Russian and U.S. immigration laws, the length and difficulty of the trip, and the fact that Eastern European Jews did not see the Southwest as the America of their dreams.

Alleviate means "to lessen."

Why would Eastern European Jewish immigrants have objected to settling in the Southwest?

Countries from which Jews emigrated in the Great Migration

Find Turkey, Poland, Lithuania, Russia, Romania, Germany, and Austria-Hungary on the map. Find out whether members of your family immigrated to the United States between 1880 and 1920. If so, where did they come from? Locate their place of origin on the map.

0   300 km

0   300 mi

Baltic Sea

Moscow

Dvinsk

Vitelbsk

Smolensk

Kovno

[LITHUANIA]

Vilno

Mogilev

Buwalki

Minsk

PRUSSIA
[GERMANY]

Grodno

Bobruysk

Gomel

Plock

Lomza Bialystok

Kalisz

[POLAND] Siedlice

Pinsk

Chernigov

RUSSIA

Lodz Warsaw

Brest-Litovsk

Plotrkow

Radom

Zhitomir

Kiev

Poltava

Kleice

Lublin

Berdichev

Kremenchug

AUSTRIA-HUNGARY

Kamenets-Podolsky

Elizavetgrad

Ekaterinoslav

Kherson

Odessa

Kishinev

[TURKEY]

Simferopol

ROMANIA

Black Sea

The Pale of Settlement

REFLECT **ON IT**

How did the lives of the Eastern European Jewish immigrants change in the United States?
How did the Eastern European Jewish immigrants change Jewish life in America?

The transition from the Old World to the New World was difficult for Eastern European Jewish immigrants. Many were poorly educated, needed work, and were willing to take almost any job that was available. They came with their families but with few possessions. They spoke Yiddish and crowded into neighborhoods that were often described as ghettoes. They were eager to acculturate and move into the middle class—or at least see their children do so. However, the many American Jews whose ancestors had arrived earlier had mixed feelings about this large influx of Eastern European Jews. They were especially concerned that the new immigrants might cause the already increasing antisemitism in America to worsen.

Acculturate means "to adopt elements of the culture or traits of another group of people."

An **influx** is an act of coming in.

GETTING STARTED

New York City's Castle Garden and, later, Ellis Island served more arriving immigrants than any other port in the United States. After obtaining permission to enter the country, many Jews found work in clothing factories and other businesses in lower Manhattan, not far from the port. The area near those factories became the first American home for about 75 percent of the Eastern European Jewish immigrants, many of whom soon settled in Harlem, upper Manhattan, and neighborhoods in Brooklyn and the Bronx.

Many of the new immigrants quickly moved to other cities, especially Chicago, Philadelphia, Boston, Saint Louis, Cleveland, and Baltimore, because they found jobs or had relatives there. Some were assisted by Jewish organizations that helped them find work in smaller cities, towns, and farming communities. B'nai B'rith, founded in 1843 by a group of New York Jews, was the first major nonreligious Jewish organization that focused on ethnic ties among Jews. Because of concern about growing antisemitism, B'nai

B'rith created the Industrial Removal Office in 1901 to move immigrants from the East Coast to smaller Jewish communities throughout the country. More than 75,000 immigrants were relocated to 1,670 cities and towns in the United States and Canada.

But the Lower East Side, as the neighborhood in lower Manhattan came to be called, remained a center for new Jewish immigrants. There, living "downtown" with and near family and friends, they enjoyed the social and religious life that the neighborhood offered. Even though many immigrants were no longer as religiously observant as they had been in Europe, a rabbi, kosher butcher, and synagogue where they could worship with a minyan were still necessities for many Jewish immigrants.

A **minyan** is a group of the ten Jewish adults required to hold a religious service. In some congregations, only men over the age of 13 can constitute a minyan.

THINK ABOUT IT What is your opinion of the effort to move immigrant Jews out of New York in order to try to reduce antisemitism? Where might you have wanted to live as a new immigrant to the United States? Why?

The Lower East Side comprised four political **wards** (the seventh, tenth, eleventh, and thirteenth), and by 1900, Jews made up 79 percent of their population. Home for most was a multistory tenement house. Many such buildings lacked light, ventilation, hot running water, baths, or private bathrooms. Jacob Riis, a photographer and journalist who became famous for documenting conditions on the Lower East Side, described a typical tenement:

"It is generally a brick building from four to six storeys high on the street, frequently with a store on the first floor; . . . four families occupy each floor, and a set of rooms consists of one or two dark closets, used as bedrooms, with a living room twelve feet by ten. The staircase is too often a dark well in the center of the house, and no direct ventilation is possible."

LEARN IT A **ward** is an administrative area of a city or town.

One immigrant described his home in these words, "Our tenement was nothing but a junk-heap of rotten lumber and brick. . . . The plaster was always falling down, the stairs broken and dirty. . . . There was no drinking water in the tenement for days. . . . The bedbugs lived and bred in the rotten walls of the tenement, with the rats, fleas, roaches. . . . In America were rooms without sunlight." [from Deborah Dwork, "Immigrant Jews on the Lower East Side of New York: 1880–1914," in *The American Jewish Experience,* ed. Jonathan D. Sarna, (New York: Holmes and Meier, 1997)]

Immigration and antisemitism

The large and rapid increase in Jewish immigration did lead to an increase in antisemitism in America. Newspapers and magazines began to publish articles in which Jews were described as "rowdy" and "strange looking." Hotels, resorts, and restaurants refused to serve Jews. This was part of a "nativist" movement, reflecting the concerns of Protestant Americans, many of whose families had lived in the United States since the seventeenth century. They were afraid of losing their jobs, their homes, and/or their political power to the new immigrants, many of whom were Catholic or Jewish.

As early as 1882, Congress had begun to regulate and restrict immigration. The first immigration law called for the exclusion of "undesirables" and people unable to take care of themselves. Laws passed in 1891 excluded immigrants whose tickets were paid for by someone else and those with "loathsome or dangerous contagious disease." Those laws created problems for Jewish immigrants and greatly increased the number of people denied permission to enter the United States.

Congress passed bills in 1897, 1913, and 1915 requiring that immigrants be **literate** in their native languages, but Presidents William McKinley, William Howard Taft, and Woodrow Wilson vetoed the legislation. Had these laws passed, they might have reduced Jewish immigration. Literacy rates among Jewish men were fairly high but among women they were lower. Also, there was no guarantee that literacy in Hebrew or Yiddish would have been acceptable to the nativists.

LEARN IT Literate means "able to read and write."

THINK ABOUT IT Should immigrants to the United States be required to be literate in their native language or in English? Why or why not?

CLICK ON IT

Learn more about the New York City tenements by visiting the Lower East Side Tenement Museum in Manhattan. Or visit the website at www.tenement.org. To see a pictorial history of the tenements, go to www.tenant.net/community/history. Or go to www.talkingstreet.com, click on "Cell Phone Walking Tour: The Lower East Side: Birthplace of Dreams," and follow the instructions ("How It Works") for taking a thirteen-stop walking tour of the neighborhood. Note there will likely be a charge on your cell phone bill for taking this tour.

THE WORKING LIFE

Most of the Jews who arrived in the United States after 1900 possessed marketable skills as manual laborers. The *shtetlach* back in Europe had provided nearby manufacturing facilities with much of their workforce, so many Jewish immigrants arrived with experience in textile and other factories. Although, Jews made up only 10 percent of the total number of immigrants to the United States during these years, they accounted for 25 percent of the skilled industrial workers entering the country. Jewish immigrants found jobs wherever they could, but the garment industry was the major field in which they found work.

Tailoring was easy to learn, and many of the immigrants, having been advised by relatives and friends who had come before them, had taken sewing lessons before leaving Europe. With New York City the center of the garment industry, some found jobs even as they were still being processed at Castle Garden or Ellis Island. This trade became increasingly attractive to newly arriving Jews because they wanted to work among other Jews. Having Jewish bosses and co-workers made life easier: The need to learn the new language was not so urgent and the freedom to observe religious laws was likely to be granted.

Jews became involved in the clothing business early on. Quite a few sold second-hand clothes, something they had done in Europe and which was not a desirable occupation in America. The industry began to grow as a

In other cities, Jewish immigrants found different types of housing, but they still usually lived in easily identifiable neighborhoods. Chicago's West Side was home to 50,000 Jews in 1900. In a commercial district close to the railroad stations, they lived in three- and four-story buildings crowded among the factories. The heart of this formerly German and Irish neighborhood was Maxwell Street, a lively center of activity with market stalls, and pushcarts among the tenements and apartment buildings. Similarly, Boston's North End, Baltimore's East Side, and South Philadelphia became immigrant neighborhoods. In some cities, the Jewish immigrants crowded in close to other new immigrants, such as the Italians.

DO IT

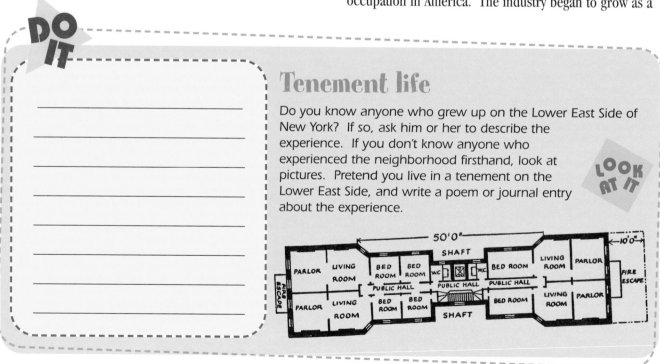

Tenement life

Do you know anyone who grew up on the Lower East Side of New York? If so, ask him or her to describe the experience. If you don't know anyone who experienced the neighborhood firsthand, look at pictures. Pretend you live in a tenement on the Lower East Side, and write a poem or journal entry about the experience.

LOOK AT IT

result of the need for uniforms during the Civil War, the invention of the sewing machine in 1846, and the large number of immigrants available to join the workforce. Because they knew the business, Jews were able to take over the production side as well. The clothing industry was one of the few industries in the United States in which Jews became employers.

Peddling was the second most common occupation among Jewish immigrants. Others found work as clerks, furriers, cigar-makers, construction workers, and shoemakers, among other occupations.

Within the garment industry, opportunity took three forms. There was the "family system," in which members of a household did "homework" in their apartment. The husband was the skilled worker, and the wife and children basted, sewed buttonholes, and did other finishing work. Working in a sweatshop meant that a contractor who spoke English would find the work, pick up the cloth or precut garments, and deliver the material to a warehouse. He then made a contract with the manufacturer to provide the finished garments at a given price by a certain date. The workers, housed in a loft or tenement apartment, filled the orders. In the "inside shops," a manufacturer worked with a designer and sold directly to a store's buyer. Regardless of its name, the workplace was usually dirty, dark, and unsanitary. The average male cloak-maker made $12 a week in 1888 but only $3.81 a week in 1904 and 1905. Female workers averaged $1.04 a week in 1904 and 1905. The weekly wages of a cloak-maker working in a sweatshop fell nearly 17 percent between 1880 and 1901, while the workday grew longer and productivity rose 66 percent.

A **sweatshop** employs workers for long hours at low wages and under poor conditions.

What do you imagine immigrant life would have been like for your family?

LIMITS TO THEIR PATIENCE

The new immigrants were willing to work hard and endure difficult living conditions. There were, however, limits to their endurance. When the price of kosher meat rose from twelve cents to eighteen cents a pound in 1902, immigrant women rioted in New York City and carried out a three-week **boycott** of kosher meat shops on the Lower East Side, and in parts of upper Manhattan, the Bronx, and Brooklyn. At first, **retail** butchers had tried to force wholesalers to lower their prices by refusing to sell meat for a week. When that strategy failed, a few women began organizing protests. Thousands of women marched through their neighborhoods, stormed into butcher shops, threw meat into the streets, and announced a boycott. About eighty-five people, mostly women, were arrested for disorderly conduct. Protesters visited synagogues to promote the boycott, and although a few rabbis opposed it, there was a great deal of support in the community.

In less than a week, the Retail Butchers Association gave in and joined the boycott against the **wholesale** meat suppliers. Orthodox rabbis soon supported it. The boycott ended when the wholesalers reduced the price of kosher meat by nine cents a pound so that retail butchers could charge fourteen cents a pound and still make a profit.

These Jewish women, many of them not yet citizens, had adopted the strategies of the newly forming labor and women's rights movements. Their example was later copied in rent strikes and other food boycotts, and many younger women, observing the success of the kosher-meat boycott, would become active in the labor movement.

A **boycott** occurs when people refuse to deal with a business.

Retail refers to the sale of goods directly to the people who use them.

Wholesale is the sale of large quantities of goods to retailers rather than consumers.

What do you think of boycotts as a tactic for creating change? Are you aware of any other boycotts? What were they and what were the results?

LEARNING TO BE AMERICANS

The Jews who had arrived a generation or more before, from Germany and other places in Central Europe, reacted to the Eastern European Jewish immigrants with mixed feelings. They were horrified by the newcomers' behavior, language, dress—in other words, they were horrified by almost everything about them. They saw the so-called Russian Jews as inferior and worried that the newcomers would quickly outnumber them. The Detroit *Jewish American* declared in an editorial in 1891: "Our great duty . . . is to raise our race. . . . The Jew . . . must elevate his lowest type, if the highest classes are to attain their legitimate place in the popular estimation. . . . It has become a question of self-defense." [from Howard M. Sachar, "Survival in the Immigrant City," in *A History of the Jews in America* (New York: Vintage Books, 1993)]

Nonetheless, the established Jews also felt responsible to help the newcomers "Americanize," partly out of self-interest and partly because the immigrants were, despite everything else, fellow Jews. Jewish leaders in many cities created educational programs, agencies, and institutions whose goals were to assist the new immigrants and teach them how to be Americans.

DO IT

In your opinion, do Jews have the obligation to help other Jews? Jews are taught that *"kol Yisrael arevim zeh ba zeh,"* "All Israel is responsible one for the other" (Babylonian Talmud, *Shavuot* 39a). What does that mean to you? List the ways in which you practice the mitzvah of taking responsibility for other Jews.

_____

_____

_____

_____

_____

Lillian Wald

Lillian Wald

Lillian Wald's interest in the medical needs of poor immigrant families on the Lower East Side of New York began with an assignment to organize a plan for home nursing during her postgraduate nursing training. She moved to the neighborhood herself in 1893 and set up an office on the top floor of a tenement building with her friend, Mary Brewster. Her practice expanded and, two years later, she moved to Henry Street, which was to be her base for forty years.

Wald and her staff helped all who needed it, regardless of race or religion. When Wald realized that children were staying home from school on account of illness, she arranged for a staff member to provide visiting-nurse services to a public school. Her solution led the New York Board of Health to organize the first public nursing system in the world. She also proposed that insurance companies provide free visiting public-health nurses to their policyholders. The Metropolitan Life Insurance Company began such a program in 1903, and other companies soon followed. Wald founded the Henry Street Settlement for the instruction of women in home nursing, cooking, and sewing, and to provide educational and recreational activities for their families.

One of the most important community centers for immigrant Jews was the Educational Alliance, organized in New York in 1889. It offered vocational courses; classes in English, civics, American history, English literature, and Greek and Roman history; public lectures; and patriotic events on national holidays.

THINK ABOUT IT

What is your opinion of the efforts by the Central European Jews to "Americanize" the new Eastern European Jewish immigrants? How do you think you would feel if you, as a new immigrant, participated in one of these programs?

What they needed to know

As early as 1875, the United Hebrew Charities, which provided supplies and services to the immigrants including food, fuel, medical care, and an employment bureau, organized classes in which girls were taught the domestic arts. The Young Men's and Young Women's Hebrew Associations (YMHA and YWHA) were also among the early organizations that helped the Eastern European Jews. The YMHA was founded in 1854 and, by 1890, had more than 120 branches. Although they had originally been established as literary and social organizations for German Jewish youths, in the 1880s the focus of their evening classes shifted to instruction in English, civics, and home economics for the new immigrants. Jacob Schiff bought a large building for the YMHA on East Ninety-second Street in New York in 1900. In other cities, too, the YMHAs offered employment services as well as recreational activities. Jewish orphanages, which had been founded in the mid-nineteenth century to serve the poor of the Central European community, also began to serve the Eastern European Jews.

Settlement houses helped Jewish and non-Jewish immigrants with medical, employment, and welfare services. Lillian Wald's Henry Street Settlement on the Lower East Side, Minnie Low's Maxwell Street Settlement House in Chicago, and Touro Hall in North Philadelphia were among the more than seventy-five settlement houses in

Learning to knit.

cities throughout the country. The settlement houses offered instruction in English, civics, and manual trades, as well as preschool preparation for immigrant children.

In some cases, well-meaning settlement-house reformers tried to persuade immigrants to acculturate by abandoning their own traditions. Some middle- and upper-class women who worked in settlement houses sought to mold the immigrants in their own image of a "proper" homemaker. They taught immigrant women how to decorate a room and set the table, skills that meant little to women who spent their days working in factories.

The domestic arts include sewing, cooking, and keeping house.

HELPING THEMSELVES

The Eastern European Jews often resented the attitudes of the "uptown" Jews, and the charity they offered, even though it was needed. As Abraham Cahan wrote, "It wasn't only the difference in our daily language and manner of speaking that got in the way. It was deeper differences in inherited concepts and customs that separated us. With the best of intentions in the world and with gentle hearts they, unknowingly, insulted us."

Thus, the Eastern European Jewish immigrants began organizing their own self-help organizations, which were more attuned to the newcomers' sensibilities than those created by the "uptowners." According to one founder of the Hebrew Sheltering Society, "It is up to us Russian Jews to help our poor countrymen, to keep them from being insulted by our proud brethren to whom a Russian Jew is a *schnorrer* [beggar], a tramp, a good-for-nothing." [from Henry L. Feingold, "The Immigration Experience of Eastern Jewry," in *Zion in America: The Jewish Experience from Colonial Times to the Present* (Mincola, New York: Dover Publications, 1981)]

What is your opinion of the reaction of the new immigrants to the help offered by the already acculturated Central European Jews?

The main self-help agencies were the *landsmanshaftn*, which were named for their members' hometowns and offered a variety of services, including education, visiting the sick, and burial. The *landsmanshaftn* also provided insurance, health services, interest-free loans, sick benefits, and social and recreational activities. They even served as employment agencies when a boss would turn to his organization to find a worker from his hometown.

The self-help principle extended to the establishment of other organizations, such as hospitals, orphanages, and nursing and old-age homes that provided kosher food and Yiddish-speaking doctors. By the late 1880s, Eastern European Jews had begun to organize their own charities. The *G'milut Hasadim* Association, the Hebrew Free Loan Society, was established in 1892 to make interest-free loans to Jewish immigrants who wanted to start businesses or needed help making ends meet. Eastern European immigrants also founded synagogues, a few yeshivas, and political organizations. By 1910, the Eastern European Jews in America had their own well-established organizational structure.

Landsmanshaftn (the plural of *landsmanshaft*) are organizations of people from the same town in Europe.

Interest-free loans are loans where only the original amount borrowed is returned to the lender. There is no additional charge to the borrower for using the loaned money.

A **yeshiva** is a school for the study of the Hebrew Bible, Talmud, and other rabbinic writings that may confer rabbinic ordination.

GETTING A GOOD EDUCATION

Education has always been a traditional Jewish value, and Jewish parents were happy to register their children in public schools in the United States. They saw free public education as one of the major blessings of the New World and the key to a modern American life. In the early 1900s, Jewish children had the lowest absentee rate in the school system.

The New York City school system was soon overwhelmed by the huge number of immigrant children, and a shift system was organized with most children

G'milut ḥesed

G'milut ḥesed is an act of loving-kindness. The rabbis say that those who perform g'milut ḥesed will be rewarded by God in this world and a second time in the next (*Shabbat* 127a). The term usually refers to a mitzvah that is performed with no thought of reward. One way of fulfilling the mitzvah is to make a loan without asking for interest. The Torah prohibits Jews from charging interest on loans to other Jews (Deuteronomy 23:20–21), although for the sake of business there is a way around the restriction. In every Jewish community, free-loan societies were set up to lend money to poor Jews. As soon as the loan was repaid, the money was lent to someone else. Why was g'milut ḥesed, especially in the form of interest-free loans, an important feature of Jewish communities?

DO IT

List ways in which you perform the mitzvah of g'milut ḥesed.

_____

_____

_____

_____

_____

_____

_____

_____

_____

_____

_____

_____

_____

_____

attending for only half a day. For many immigrant Jewish children, school ended at sixth or, sometimes, eighth grade, when they went to work to help support their families. Most of these children learned to read and write. Teachers attempting to acculturate them also taught a great deal about personal cleanliness, correct English pronunciation, and citizenship.

Although not all Jewish immigrants were religiously observant, many respected their tradition and wanted their children to receive a Jewish education. On the Lower East Side, girls generally attended the Hebrew Free School Association while boys went to a traditional *ḥeder*. A few boys attended day schools in order to study Talmud. Most Jewish children did not receive a Jewish education, however.

Education was also crucial for adults. Jewish men were far less likely than other immigrants to be illiterate, yet Jewish women were almost twice as likely as Jewish men to be illiterate. In night schools, which were well attended by Jewish women, adults studied English and civics. Although private colleges discriminated against Jews, public colleges were open to all students with good enough grades. Medicine was a favorite profession, as were careers in law, teaching, dentistry, and pharmacy. So many of the students of the City College of New York were Jewish that the school earned the nickname the "Jewish College of America." Jews called it the "poor man's Harvard."

A *ḥeder* is a supplementary school for learning Hebrew and other Judaic studies.

Teach it to your children. In the Torah we read, "You shall teach it [Torah] to your children" (Deuteronomy 6:7). There are many other verses in the Torah and the Talmud that speak of the importance of education. Find several of them, and write a *d'var Torah* explaining why education is so highly valued in the Jewish community.

Why is receiving a Jewish education important to your family?

CULTURE IN THE GHETTO

Information was also to be had through other means. Although Yiddish was looked down upon by the "uptowners," the "downtowners" valued the Yiddish press as a window into the happenings in America and the world. Before 1914, more than 150 weekly, monthly, and quarterly journals were published in Yiddish. Most important, however, were the Yiddish daily newspapers, all of which were published in New York. They were circulated nationally, so Jewish immigrants in Baltimore, Philadelphia, Boston, Chicago, Detroit, Cleveland, and almost every other large American city read a New York Yiddish paper. The Yiddish newspapers printed works of European Jewish authors and Yiddish translations of European classics. Local journalists wrote about life on the Lower East Side.

The largest and most important of these papers was the *Forverts* (the *Forward*), which began in 1897 and, within a decade, became the largest Yiddish newspaper in the world. Its editor from 1901 to 1951 was Abraham Cahan, who saw himself as an educator as well as a journalist. While many of the Yiddish newspapers were full of stories of crime and violence, Cahan made sure that articles in his paper were interesting, relevant, and well written. And since he believed it was his duty to educate his fellow immigrants in the ways of American life, the *Forverts* carried the "Bintel Brief" ("bundle or collection of letters"), a Yiddish advice column that was the paper's most popular feature. Immigrants wrote to the "Bintel Brief" columnist about everything from love to money to jobs. Every letter was answered, if not in the paper then by Cahan himself or by another editor.

Yiddish theater was established in 1882 in America, with the first Yiddish production on the Lower East Side only six years after the first Yiddish play in Europe was staged in Romania. It gave many immigrants their first taste of entertainment, a break from the rough life they were living. The first performances were mostly comedies.

The Yiddish Dear Abby

Here is a sampling of letters from the "Bintel Brief":

Letter: "I am a young man of twenty-five, and I recently met a fine girl. She has a flaw, however—a dimple in her chin. It is said that people who have this lose their first husband or wife. I love her very much. But I'm afraid to marry her lest I die because of the dimple."

Answer: "The tragedy is not that the girl has a dimple in her chin but that some people have a screw loose in their heads."

Letter: "My dearest friends of the Forward, I have been jobless for six months now. I have eaten the last shirt on my back and now there is nothing left for me. . . .

Answer: "This is one of hundreds of heartrending pleas for help, cries of need, that we receive daily. The writer of this letter should go first to the Crisis Conference [address given], and they will not let him starve. And further, we ask our readers to let us know if someone can create a job for this unemployed man."

CLICK ON IT Go to "Learning Adventures in Citizenship at www.pbs.org/wnet/newyork/laic." Click on episode 4 and then click on "The Bintel Brief" to see more letters.

DO IT Write two or three of your own questions and answers to the "Bintel Brief." Try to ask questions about matters that would have concerned the immigrant Jews of the early 1900s.

The quality of Yiddish theater in America improved in 1891, with the arrival in the United States of the playwright Jacob Gordin and the formation of an acting company by the actor-director Jacob Adler. Adler's dream was to perform "only beautiful musical operas and dramas giving truthful and serious portrayals of life." He therefore chose to perform only Gordin's plays, and it was the presentation of Gordin's Jewish King Lear that gave Yiddish theater the reputation of serious art. Other playwrights soon followed, and by 1917 Yiddish theater companies were performing in Boston, Philadelphia, Baltimore, Chicago, and Los Angeles.

 THINK ABOUT IT In your opinion, why did Yiddish theater become so popular? Why was it important to the Eastern European immigrants?

JEWISH FAMILY LIFE

With education and acculturation to American life came greater tensions within many families—between husbands and wives and between parents and children. Men who often arrived first and, therefore, had a head start generally adapted to their new lives more quickly than their wives, especially if the husband had more opportunities to venture beyond the neighborhood. They tended to argue over knowledge of English, styles of clothing, the wearing of wigs (a custom among observant Jewish women), and other practices. Marital relations were also strained by financial problems, poor living conditions, long hours of work and, in many immigrant households, the presence of boarders.

 LEARN IT **Boarders** are people who pay to live and eat in someone's home.

As children became integrated into American society, through what they learned in school, in settlement-house activities, or on the street, they came into conflict with their parents whom they considered old-fashioned. Children often neglected traditional religious practices, wanted more independence, and felt ashamed of their parents' Old World ways and poor English. As one female character in a semi-autobiographical novel by a daughter of immigrants complained, "I dressed her [her mother] in the most stylish Paris models, but Delancey Street sticks out from every inch of her. Whenever she opens her mouth, I'm done for. I, with all my style and pep, can't get a man my equal because a girl is always judged by her mother."

The parents, for their part, often did not understand their Americanized children. One father wrote to the *Forward* about his son's love of baseball: "What is the point of the crazy game? It makes sense to teach a child to play dominoes or chess. But baseball? The children can get crippled. . . . I want my boy to grow up to be a mensch, not a wild American runner." In response, Abraham Cahan wrote that Jewish boys should be permitted to play baseball as long as it does not interfere with their education. [from Irving Howe, *World of Our Fathers* (New York and London: Harcourt, Brace and Jovanovich, 1976)]

AMERICANS ALL

Slowly but surely, the Eastern European Jewish immigrants established themselves in the United States. They developed a unique and vibrant culture that celebrated their heritage while embracing their adopted home. And they had a lasting effect on that home, reinforcing the Jewish identity of Jews throughout the country.

By the mid-twentieth century, the negative feelings that had sometimes existed between the German and Russian Jews largely disappeared. Descendants of Central European Jews and descendants of Eastern European Jews had begun to marry one another, work together, and share the responsibility of supporting the American Jewish community.

DO IT Watch the movie *Hester Street*. Based on the short novel, *Yekl*, by Abraham Cahan, it focuses on marital conflict caused by differences in acculturation and on the role of a boarder in the household. How does the movie depict daily life in the tenements? What does it show about the pressures on immigrant Jewish families during this time?

Yiddish theater poster

CHAPTER 6
JEWS IN THE RANKS OF LABOR

Why did Jews become so involved in the labor movement?
What were some of their most important contributions to the movement?

- -

Although Jews still made up only a small percentage of the U.S. population, they played an important role in the national labor movement that sprang to life in the late nineteenth and early twentieth centuries. With industrialization and the growth of factory production, laborers began to organize and demand improvements in working conditions. Jewish labor leaders helped to create unions that served both Jewish and non-Jewish workers. They fought for higher wages, shorter hours, and healthier conditions in the garment and other industries, and introduced many programs that enriched workers' lives.

SEEDS SOWN IN EUROPE

Many of the Eastern European Jewish immigrants who came to the United States after 1905 were very different from those who had come before. More of them had lived in large cities and worked in factories in Europe. Many had read the works of Russian and German writers, had experienced the growth of Yiddish literature and theater, and had broken away from their parents' strictly traditional form of religious observance. Quite a few of them had been involved in the socialist movement that was sweeping through Eastern Europe. By the early 1900s, thousands of young Jewish workers in Russia and Poland had organized into the Bund, formally known as the General Jewish Workers' Union. Suffering as workers and as Jews, they participated in strikes, sabotage, and even violence against the government. Socialism became the main political force in Eastern European Jewish life.

Although a few Jewish immigrants of the time supported anarchism, most were offended by the anarchists' violence and contempt for Jewish religious traditions, and they embraced socialism instead. In the United States, the Socialist Party appealed to Jews because it emphasized economic justice and the rights of workers, and because Jews were allowed to register in their own Yiddish-language federations. The party also had a large number of members who had been born in America, and they lent it some respectability. By 1910, the Socialist Party was active on the Lower East Side, and socialism was about to reach the height of its influence in the nation. For many Jews, socialism and Judaism, with their emphasis on fellowship and humanitarianism, blended neatly. Even though many Jewish immigrants now had a secular orientation, they may have been influenced by traditional Jewish values such as *tzedakah*, social justice, and *tikun olam*.

Socialism is a political system in which everyone owns a share of the means of production and the goods that are produced. Ideally, socialism does not allow for individual business owners or for vast differences in individuals' incomes. In most socialist countries, however, the ideal is not achieved.

Anarchism is a political theory that opposes all forms of government.

Humanitarianism is the concern for the good of humanity.

Tikun olam means "repair of the world." It refers to the Jewish idea that every person, in partnership with God, is responsible for helping to make the world a better place.

Working in a sweatshop.

THE RISE OF THE AMERICAN LABOR MOVEMENT

At the turn of the century, the wealthiest 2 percent of American families owned more than one-third of the nation's wealth. Their mansions and lavish lifestyles were in stark contrast to the tenements and simple pleasures of working people. At the same time, business owners' drive for profits produced conflicts between workers and management. The typical worker labored fifty-nine hours a week, and many worked a seven-day, eighty-four-hour week. The average hourly wage was just over twenty-one cents, and the average annual earnings were $644. Workers also faced seasonal unemployment and were fined for lateness and other "offenses." Sweatshops often paid by the piece instead of by the hour, in effect forcing workers to labor long hours to earn a meager living. In some industries, workers were required to pay for their own machines and supplies. In addition to the financial hardships, laborers suffered from poor working conditions: Workrooms were hot and poorly ventilated and the machinery was dangerous. The culture of the time respected the rights of factory owners much more than the rights of laborers.

JEWISH WORKERS WANT JEWISH UNIONS

Organizing workers into unions was a difficult undertaking, especially among the Eastern European Jewish immigrants. The sweatshops in which most of them worked were too small to encourage such organization. The "sweaters," or contractors, who brought the work were

their employers, and most workers never saw the shops' owners. During the busy season, there was full employment, but in slower times the bosses would hire inexperienced laborers, who would work for less money, and they would lay others off. The new immigrants, grateful for any job, especially one provided by a *landsman* (someone from their old *shtetl*), were unwilling to do anything to upset what they saw as their good fortune.

Although there were a few successful strikes of Jewish cap-makers, cigar-makers, and men's coat tailors in New York and Chicago during the 1870s, once the crisis that led to the strike was over, the workers seemed to lose interest and their unions disappeared. The gains they made were lost. Finally, however, as factories began to employ more laborers directly, workers had the opportunity to organize. Angry at the terrible conditions under which they worked, especially since they had expected more from life in America, the immigrants of the Lower East Side began to take action.

Non-Jewish unions did not welcome immigrants in general and Eastern European Jewish workers in particular. Jewish leaders decided, therefore, that they needed their own unions. In 1888, Morris Hillquit and several other Lower East Side Jews founded a labor federation called the United Hebrew Trades. Born Moshe Hilkowitz in Riga, Latvia, Hillquit arrived in the United States in 1886 at the age of seventeen, worked in the garment industry for a short time, and then became a union organizer.

The United Hebrew Trades was intended to encourage union organizing among all working Jews in the garment industry and in other "Jewish" industries. Over the next two years, almost forty unions were brought into the federation, including a shirtmakers' union, a knee-pants-makers' union, a cloak-makers' union, a cap-makers' union, a bakers' union, and a Yiddish-actors' union. Yet maintaining the unions was difficult, at least in part because Jews did not intend to remain in the working class for long.

THINK ABOUT IT What is your opinion of the need for Jewish unions?

The American Federation of Labor (which merged with the Congress of Industrial Organizations in 1955 to form the AFL-CIO) was organized in 1886. It admitted only skilled workers and preferred strikes to political action. Its main goal was economic gain, and each union within the federation retained a great deal of power. Its leader, Samuel Gompers, was Jewish and had attended a free Jewish school until age ten, when he became a shoemaker's apprentice. He came to the United States from London as a teenager in 1863 and worked in his father's trade of cigar-making. He helped found the Cigarmakers Union, becoming its president in 1877.

Gompers helped negotiate the organization of the AFL and was chosen to be its first president. Dedicated to the rights of the worker, he helped lead the fight against sweatshops and succeeded in winning battles for decent wages and an eight-hour workday. In 1894, Gompers helped persuade Congress to designate the first Monday in September as Labor Day, a national holiday. By the time he died, in 1924, the AFL had grown to 5 million members. The U.S. Post Office issued a commemorative stamp in his honor in 1950, on the centennial of his birth.

UNREST IN THE GARMENT INDUSTRY

The garment industry was the main focus of Jewish labor protests because so many Jewish immigrants worked in that industry. Understanding that a national union would be more powerful than a single local group, representatives of local unions created the International Ladies Garment Workers Union (ILGWU) on June 3, 1900. It was granted a charter by the AFL and grew quickly; only four years later, its membership included sixty-six local unions. Despite its name, the organization's membership

A notable quotation by David Dubinsky

"Yes, we were dreamers when we advocated legislation for unemployment insurance, for social security, for minimum wages. They laughed at our crazy ideas. Although we have not reached perfection, many of our 'wild dreams' have now become realities of everyday life."

DO IT While the issues Dubinsky names were important later, the issues of the early twentieth century were child labor, the length of the workday, and workplace safety. Do some research on these issues. Why were they important?

"*I went to work for the Triangle Shirtwaist Company in 1901. The corner of a shop would resemble a kindergarten because we were young, eight, nine, ten years old. . . . The hours were from 7:30 in the morning to 6:30 at night when it wasn't busy. . . . No overtime pay, not even supper money. There was a bakery in the garment center that produced little apple pies . . . and that was what we got for our overtime instead of money.*

"*My wages as a youngster were $1.50 for a seven-day week. I know it sounds exaggerated, but it isn't. . . . When the operators were through with sewing shirtwaists, there was a little thread left, and we youngsters would get a little scissors and trim the threads off.*

"*And when the inspectors came around, . . . the supervisors made all the children climb into one of those crates that they ship material in, and they covered us over with finished shirtwaists until the inspectors had left, because of course we were too young to be working in the factory legally.*

"*The Triangle Shirtwaist Company was a family affair, all relatives of the owner running the place, watching to see that you did your work, watching when you went into the toilet. And if you were two or three minutes longer than foremen or foreladies thought you should be, it was deducted from your pay. If you came five minutes late in the morning because the freight elevator didn't come down to take you up in time, you were sent home for a half a day without pay.*

"*The early sweatshops were usually so dark that gas jets (for light) burned day and night. There was no insulation in the winter, only a pot-bellied stove in the middle of the factory. . . . Of course in summer you suffocated with practically no ventilation. There was no drinking water, maybe a tap in the hall, warm, dirty. What were you going to do? Drink this water or none at all.*

"*Someone asked me once: 'How did you survive?' And I told him, 'What alternative did we have?' You stayed and you survived, that's all.*"

At right above, a widow and her son roll papers for cigarettes in a New York City tenement.
At right below, a Jewish woman and her daughters make garters for the Liberty Garter works.

A first-person account

Pauline Newman, who worked for the Triangle Shirtwaist Company and became a leader in the ILGWU, wrote about the conditions in the factories.

["Working at the Triangle Shirtwaist Company" adapted by the Lower Hudson Regional Information Center from the Berkeley Parents Network, "UCB Parents Advice About Holidays and Special Events: International Women's Day."]

CLICK ON IT

Click on www.lhric.org/wh/wh2.html to read more.

LOOK AT IT

was two-thirds male and the union's founders were all Jewish men.

One prominent leader of the ILGWU was David Dubinsky. After growing up in the Russian-ruled section of Poland, Dubinsky was exiled to a Siberian prison in 1908 for his labor activities. He escaped and came to the United States in 1911. A Socialist, he worked as a cloak-maker and joined the ILGWU. He rose quickly through the ranks of the union, serving as its president for thirty-four years and making it one of the most powerful unions in America.

Conditions in the garment industry remained harsh. Workers at two of the shirtwaist (blouse) shops were already on strike on November 22, 1909. On that day, in a meeting at New York's Cooper Union College led by AFL president Samuel Gompers, thousands of women, members of the ILGWU, met to discuss whether to call an industry-wide strike of all the shops. A young woman named Clara Lemlich spoke these now-famous words: "I am a working girl . . . I am tired of listening to speakers . . . What we are here for is to decide whether or not to strike. I offer a resolution that a general strike be declared—now!"

The strike, which the newspapers called the Uprising of the 20,000, was declared. It was the largest strike by women in the United States up to that time. Jewish women made up two-thirds of the workers in the industry and were leaders of both organizers and strikers. The women protested the fifty-six-hour workweek, during which they usually earned less than six dollars. Business leaders asked the police to treat the strikers harshly, and 723 women were arrested. Supporting the strikers were the Women's Trade Union League, an organization of mostly middle-class, non-Jewish women; college students who raised money for the strikers; and wealthy women who joined them on the picket lines and became known as "the mink brigade." Raising money was essential because during a strike the workers and their families often went hungry.

The strike ended on February 15, 1910, with the *Forverts* declaring that "the big fight has ended. The huge general strike of the ladies . . . is won." But although the workers returned to their jobs having won shorter hours and better wages, the shops remained "open," with employers hiring nonunion workers. Moreover, the manufacturers did not recognize the ILGWU as the official representative of the garment workers. This victory was,

therefore, limited. Union membership grew in the year after the strike, however, and the action inspired a number of other major strikes.

Just five months later, on July 7, male workers in the cloak-makers industry formed picket lines. In what would be dubbed the Great Revolt, between 50,000 and 60,000 men left their jobs in a well-organized effort on both the local and the national level. The strike affected 1,800 shops and involved mostly Jewish-owned shops, Jewish workers, and a minority of Italian workers.

The Great Revolt ended on September 2 with the workers being granted most of their demands. The mediators were leaders of the Jewish community, including Louis D. Brandeis, who would later be appointed to the Supreme

A reporter writes about the strike

McAlister Coleman, a reporter for the *New York Sun*, watched the strikers and later described the incident he witnessed:

"The girls, headed by teen-age Clara Lemlich, described by union organizers as a 'pint of trouble for the bosses,' began singing Italian and Russian working-class songs as they paced in twos before the factory door. All of a sudden, around the corner came a dozen tough-looking customers, for whom the union label 'gorillas' seemed well-chosen.

"'Stand fast, girls,' called Clara, and then the thugs rushed the line, knocking Clara to her knees, striking at the pickets, opening the way for a group of frightened scabs to slip through the broken line . . . There was a confused melee of scratching, screaming girls and fist-swinging men and then a patrol wagon arrived. The thugs ran off as the cops pushed Clara and two other badly beaten girls into the wagon.

"I followed the rest of the retreating pickets to the union hall . . . There a relief station had been set up where one bottle of milk and a loaf of bread were given to strikers with small children in their families. There for the first time in my comfortably sheltered, Upper West Side life, I saw real hunger on the faces of my fellow Americans in the richest city in the world."

from Irving Howe, *World of Our Fathers* (New York: Harcourt Brace Jovanovich, 1976)

Court, and Jacob Schiff and Louis Marshall of the American Jewish Committee. What impressed Brandeis was that Jews on both sides were willing to listen to and negotiate with each other.

The "Protocol of Peace" agreement established a preferential union shop, meaning that union members would be hired before nonunion members were hired. It established a board of arbitration, which would include a member of the union, a representative of the manufacturers, and a member of the public, to negotiate major disputes; a board of grievances to settle minor complaints; and a joint board of sanitary control to advocate for decent working conditions. In addition, it established a fifty-hour workweek, "time and a half" pay for overtime, ten fully paid legal holidays, and a regularly scheduled payday. The precedent-setting settlement was the ILGWU's first major victory.

A **protocol** is the original draft from which a treaty is prepared.

Arbitration is a process in which a neutral individual settles a dispute.

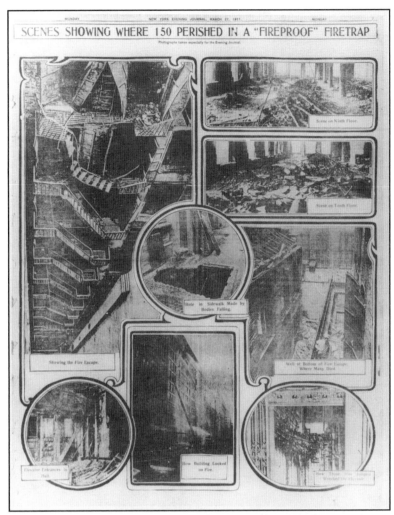

A newspaper account of the Triangle Shirtwaist Factory fire.

The historian Lucy Dawidowicz points out that Judaism emphasizes positive attitudes toward work. She writes that our tradition "endows labor with divine attributes" in that the people of Israel were commanded to work on six days, just as they were commanded to rest on the seventh day. How would this attitude toward work affect both employers and employees?

A TRAGEDY HIGHLIGHTS THE PROBLEMS

Less than one year after the major strikes of 1910, the many problems that still existed in the clothing industry were brought to light in a tragic way. On Saturday, March 25, 1911, a fire broke out in the Triangle Shirtwaist Factory, a nonunion shop located on the top three floors of a ten-story building not far from Washington Square in New York City. About 500 women and girls, mostly Jewish and

Italian immigrants, worked there making shirtwaists from a lightweight fabric. The managers had locked the doors to the stairways, supposedly to prevent theft but also leaving workers with no means of escape. Within minutes, the building was engulfed in flames. Firemen's ladders could not reach beyond the sixth floor. Some workers were able to find their way to open staircases and others were caught in nets the firemen held below, but forty-six women leaped to their death and 100 more died in the building.

The owners of the building were tried for manslaughter but were acquitted when jurors could not agree on whether they had ordered the doors to be locked or had not known that they were locked. Union leaders pressured the New York State legislature to pass significant reforms, including a fifty-four-hour workweek, improved safety regulations, and the requirement that workers be at least fifteen years old. By the end of 1911, the city of New York had set up a Bureau of Fire Investigation to establish and enforce safety regulations. Unions began to improve workers' living conditions by building cooperative housing and providing education, medical care, and insurance.

THE TRAGEDY'S AFTERMATH

A year after the Triangle Shirtwaist tragedy, 10,000 furriers launched a general strike, which was settled through the efforts of Rabbi Judah Magnes. Memories of the Triangle Shirtwaist Fire made the public more sympathetic to strikes by female-dominated unions in the garment industry.

Many Jews hoped to leave the working class and aspired to become factory owners. By the 1890s, Eastern European Jews had begun to take over the ownership of some manufacturing facilities from Central European Jews. As Jews entered the middle class, however, the Jewish labor movement declined. Over the years, an unusual peace developed between workers and employers, perhaps because the majority of both groups were Jews.

DO IT

Conduct an interview. Speak to a parent, teacher, or other adult to learn about his or her experiences as a member of a union or in a nonunionized job. If you interview a union member, list some of the benefits and workplace regulations that the union has made possible. If you interview a non-unionized worker, find out about the labor practices in his or her workplace.

_____

_____

_____

_____

_____

_____

_____

During the relatively short time when many Jews were active in the labor movement, Jewish labor leaders and workers made significant contributions. They won better pay and improved working conditions. In addition, the Jewish unions pioneered programs that provided additional benefits, such as **pensions**, medical care, unemployment and health insurance, low-interest banking, credit unions, affordable housing, educational programs, and vacations. They also made financial contributions to a variety of causes, both Jewish and secular. Many Americans have benefited from the Jewish workers'

Fania Mary Cohn: Labor leader

An important leader of the ILGWU was Fania Mary Cohn, who gave women a voice in the labor movement. Born in 1885 in Russia, she immigrated to New York City with her family in 1904. Cohn took a job as a sleeve-maker in a garment factory and was soon elected to the executive board of a local chapter of the Wrapper, Kimono, and House Dress Makers' Union of the ILGWU. As an organizer for the ILGWU, she led the first successful strike of Chicago's dress and white-goods (domestic linens) workers in 1915.

When she returned to New York, Cohn was appointed to the ILGWU'S General Education Committee and then became the executive secretary of the Education Department. She expanded the program, making it the largest education department in any union in the country.

Cohn believed strongly in the importance of education as a way to create union loyalty and instill in workers a "social conscience." In the February 1934 issue of the _American Federalist_, she wrote: "While organization gives the workers power, purposeful, dynamic education gives them the ability to use that power intelligently and effectively."

THINK ABOUT IT Do you agree with Cohn about the importance of education for laborers? Why or why not?

willingness to fight for a better life and their employers' eventual willingness to make peace and improve working conditions.

A **pension** is a set amount of money paid regularly by a former employer to a retired or disabled person who has met certain requirements.

Do people today continue to work under poor conditions in the United States? In other countries? What strikes, boycotts, or protests are you aware of today? What were the causes and the results? What do you think of them?

Judaism teaches a great deal about how employers should treat workers and how workers should behave toward their employers. In Deuteronomy (24:14–15), we read: "You shall not abuse a needy and destitute laborer, whether a fellow countryman or a stranger . . . You must pay him his wages on the same day, before the sun sets, for he is needy and urgently depends on it: let him not cry to the Lord against you and you will incur guilt." And in the Jerusalem Talmud (*Demai* 7:4), we read: "A man must not . . . work at his own affairs at night, and hire himself out by day. And he must not undertake fasts or other . . . deprivations, because the ensuing weakness will diminish the amount of work he can perform for his employer." What is the meaning of these quotes? Can you think of examples that illustrate the situations they describe?

In the Tanach or other Jewish sources, find additional quotations about good labor practices. Write them below.

_____

_____

_____

_____

_____

_____

_____

_____

Word Find

In the box find the following names of people and places that we read about in Unit 2:

Cohn	Lower East Side
Lazarus	Marshall
Cahan	Gompers
Goldman	Dubinsky
Wald	Galveston
Ellis Island	Schiff

Ask your teacher to check your answers in the Teaching Guide.

```
S E B Y R U P M K E R S D M
D E T G B Q U I N K P L E A
X E S C H I F F V E R H E R
L O C N U O T C S E C Y O S
R G H O E Y K S N I B U D H
P O N T H W C D E T R O G A
M L E X O N O L W A R E A L
E D I S T S A E R E W O L L
V M D S U O I T D F A D V B
J A E V F R T I W O L F E K
I N R S W C A R T Y D B S Q
G O M P E R S Z D E Y O T N
C E A M U N A H A C R W O P
S D N A L S I S I L L E N A
```

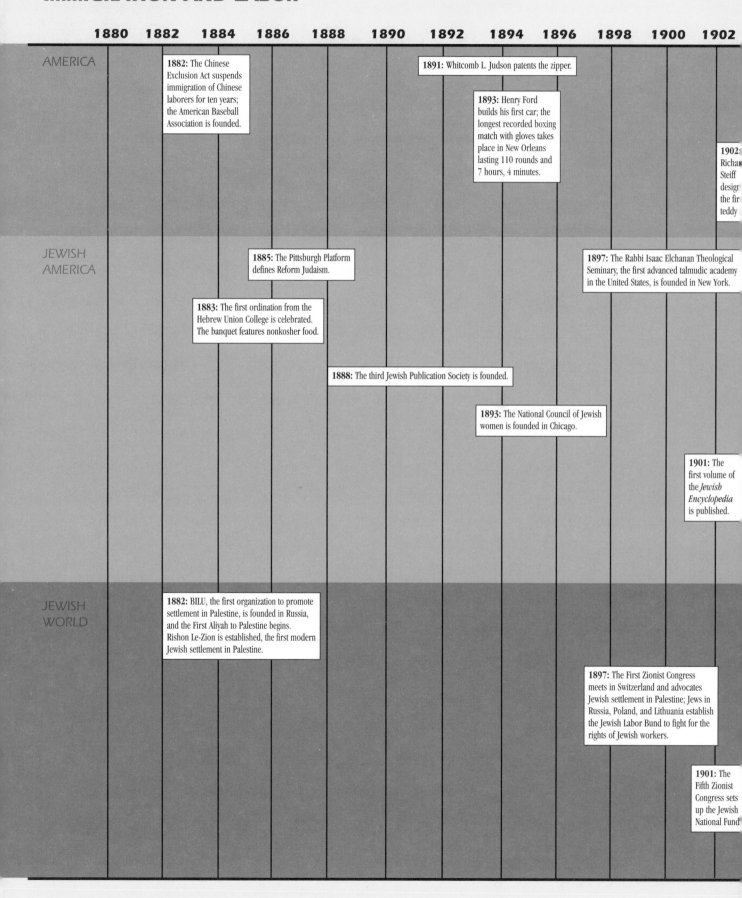

	1880	1882	1884	1886	1888	1890	1892	1894	1896	1898	1900	1902

AMERICA

1882: The Chinese Exclusion Act suspends immigration of Chinese laborers for ten years; the American Baseball Association is founded.

1891: Whitcomb L. Judson patents the zipper.

1893: Henry Ford builds his first car; the longest recorded boxing match with gloves takes place in New Orleans lasting 110 rounds and 7 hours, 4 minutes.

1902: Richa... Steiff desig... the fir... teddy

JEWISH AMERICA

1885: The Pittsburgh Platform defines Reform Judaism.

1883: The first ordination from the Hebrew Union College is celebrated. The banquet features nonkosher food.

1888: The third Jewish Publication Society is founded.

1893: The National Council of Jewish women is founded in Chicago.

1897: The Rabbi Isaac Elchanan Theological Seminary, the first advanced talmudic academy in the United States, is founded in New York.

1901: The first volume of the *Jewish Encyclopedia* is published.

JEWISH WORLD

1882: BILU, the first organization to promote settlement in Palestine, is founded in Russia, and the First Aliyah to Palestine begins. Rishon Le-Zion is established, the first modern Jewish settlement in Palestine.

1897: The First Zionist Congress meets in Switzerland and advocates Jewish settlement in Palestine; Jews in Russia, Poland, and Lithuania establish the Jewish Labor Bund to fight for the rights of Jewish workers.

1901: The Fifth Zionist Congress sets up the Jewish National Fund

1904   1906   1908   1910   1912   1914   1916   1918   1920   1922   1924   1926

1904: The first subway line opens in New York City; Helen Keller, who is deaf and blind, graduates from Radcliffe College.

1910: Father's Day is first celebrated.

1916: Washington State College defeats Brown University in the first Rose Bowl football game; a law establishing an eight-hour workday for railroad workers heads off a nationwide strike. Wilson is reelected.

1905: Albert Einstein formulates the theory of relativity and the quantum theory of light.

1919: President Wilson presides over the first League of Nations meeting in Paris and wins the Nobel Peace Prize.

1908: The Ford Motor Company produces the first Model T; Wilbur Wright flies an aircraft thirty miles in forty minutes.

1920: The Westinghouse Electric and Manufacturing Company begins the first national radio broadcasting station in the United States.

1906: President Roosevelt appoints Oscar Straus secretary of commerce and labor, making him the first Jew to serve in the cabinet.

1912: The United States lets a trade treaty with Russia expire because of Russia's refusal to honor the passports of American Jews; Henrietta Szold founds Hadassah, the Women's Zionist Organization of America.

1920: Henry Ford's *Dearborn Independent* begins publishing articles describing a supposed international Jewish conspiracy based on *The Protocols of the Elders of Zion,* an antisemitic forgery.

1904: Temple Beth El in Detroit replaces assigned seats with a system allowing congregants to sit where they choose.

1913: The murder trial of Leo Frank in Atlanta leads to the founding of the Anti-Defamation League of B'nai B'rith; Solomon Schechter founds the United Synagogue of America.

1922: Mordecai Kaplan founds the Society for the Advancement of Judaism; Harvard's president proposes a quota on the number of Jews admitted to the university.

1907: Physicist Albert Michelson becomes the first American Jew to win a Nobel Prize.

1915: Leo Frank is kidnapped and lynched after his death sentence is commuted to life imprisonment by the governor of Georgia; Moses Alexander, elected governor of Idaho, becomes the first Jewish governor in the United States.

1925: Edna Ferber becomes the first American Jew to win a Pulitzer Prize in fiction.

1909: Julius Rosenwald begins to promote the growth of Sears, Roebuck and Company. In the 1930s it became the largest mail-order house in the world.

1918: In a published letter, President Wilson approves of the Zionist program and the Balfour Declaration, favoring the establishment of a Jewish homeland in Palestine.

1904: Herzl is unsuccessful in an effort to persuade Pope Pius X to support Zionism.

1920: Adolf Hitler becomes the head of an antisemitic political party; Tel Hai in Palestine falls to Arab attackers.

1905: The Seventh Zionist Congress declines an offer of a Jewish settlement in East Africa. Gimnazia Herzilia, the first Hebrew high school, opens in Tel Aviv; the settlers of the Second Aliyah begin to arrive in Palestine.

1921: Rabbis Abraham Isaac Kook and Yaakov Meir are elected the first two chief rabbis of Israel.

1909: Degania, the first kibbutz, and Ha-Shomer, a Jewish self-defense organization, are founded in Palestine.

1922: Great Britain is granted the mandate for Palestine by the League of Nations, and Transjordan is set up on three-quarters of the land.

1917: General Edmund Allenby takes over the British command of Palestine and captures Jerusalem from the Ottomans; Jews support revolution in Russia as a solution to oppression.

CHAPTER 7
THE BEGINNING

How did events around the world affect the growth of Zionism in the United States?

Can you imagine a time when the State of Israel did not exist? Not very long ago, Jews did not have a land to call their own. There was no home for Jewish immigrants escaping persecution, no place where Jews could lead a full religious life and create a unique Jewish culture. Israel is that place. It was born in 1948, but the seeds that gave birth to it were planted many years before.

Zionism

The term Zionism, which was invented in the late nineteenth century by a man named Nathan Birnbaum, comes from *Tziyon* [Zion], the name the biblical prophets called Jerusalem. Ever since, it has been used by Jews to mean the Holy Land. Over the years, many Jews in America and throughout the world became Zionists, supporters of the movement to build a Jewish state in the land known as Palestine.

DO IT

The hope that Jews would return to Zion is expressed in many Jewish prayers and rituals. The Passover seder concludes with the declaration *"l'shanah haba'ah B'Yrushalayim."* "Next year in Jerusalem." How many times can you find the words *Zion,* or *Jerusalem,* or other references to the Land of Israel in the Shabbat evening or morning service in a *siddur* (prayer book)? What other rituals that remind Jews of their devotion to Israel and Jerusalem can you identify?

IN THE BEGINNING

After the destruction of the Second Temple by the Romans in 70 CE, the Jews were scattered throughout the world, and a long line of conquerors, including Romans, Muslim Arabs, and Ottoman Turks, ruled the Land of Israel. Yet Jews always hoped and prayed for the time that the land would be theirs again. And they always supported the small groups of Jews who remained in Palestine even when other peoples ruled the land.

Theodor Herzl, a Jewish journalist from Vienna, is universally known as the Father of Zionism. However, Mordecai Manuel Noah, a journalist, politician, and leader of the American Jewish community, spoke of a Jewish homeland many years before Herzl did. Concerned about the suffering of Jews throughout the world, in the early 1820s Noah decided to found a settlement on

Theodor Herzl, the father of Zionism

Grand Island, near Buffalo, New York, for Jews who were persecuted in Europe. He named it Ararat, for the mountain where the biblical Noah's ark came to rest after the flood. The modern Noah saw his settlement as a place to prepare Jews for their later return to Palestine.

Noah tried to persuade "Jewish bankers or other wealthy and respectable persons" to immigrate to Ararat. He held an elaborate dedication ceremony, to which he invited local Indians, whom he believed were members of one of the lost tribes of Israel. Dressed as King Richard III in an elaborate costume borrowed from a local theater, Noah proclaimed Ararat a "city of refuge" for Jews and appointed himself "judge of Israel." In a "proclamation to the Jews," he proposed, among other things, that every Jew in the world be taxed "three shekels of silver" to support the Jewish nation and for the Paris Jewish Consistory to elect a judge every four years based on proxy votes from every congregation of Jews in the world. A cornerstone was laid that contained the *Sh'ma* in Hebrew and the inscription "ARARAT. A city of Refuge for the Jews. Founded by Mordecai Manuel Noah in the month of Tizri 5586 Sept. 1825 and in the 50th year of American Independence." [from Jonathan D. Sarna, *Jacksonian Jew: The Two Worlds of Mordecai Noah* (New York: Holmes and Meier, 1980)]

Not only did Noah fail to attract settlers, he was ridiculed by people around the world. However, he later spoke about Jewish settlers in Palestine to audiences of both Jews and Christians. Although there was some interest in Noah's ideas, most Jews were not prepared to establish a separate Jewish colony in America or return to the land of Israel.

 A **consistory** was a Jewish communal organization in France which regulated religious and communal affairs as well as relations with the government.

A vote by **proxy** is a vote by someone who is authorized to act for someone else.

 Why might Noah have believed that Americans would support Ararat? Would you have supported Ararat? Why or why not?

Mordecai Manuel Noah and John Adams

Mordecai Manuel Noah

In 1819, Mordecai Manuel Noah sent John Adams, the second president of the United States, a copy of his newly published book, *Travels in England, France, Spain, and the Barbary States.* Adams praised the gift, saying that he wished that Noah had been able to tour Syria, Judea and Jerusalem. He wrote, ". . . I . . . wish that you had been at the head of a hundred thousand Israelites . . . marching with them into Judea & making a conquest of that country & restoring your nation to the dominion of it. For I really wish the Jews again in Judea an independent nation."

In the next sentence, however, Adams added: "I believe [that] . . . once restored to an independent government & no longer persecuted they [the Jews] would soon wear away some of the asperities and peculiarities of their character & possibly in time become liberal Unitarian Christians for your Jehovah is our Jehovah & your God of Abraham, Isaac and Jacob is our God." [from Michael Feldberg, ed. *Blessings of Freedom: Chapters in American Jewish History* (Hoboken, New Jersey: KTAV Publishing House and the American Jewish Historical Society, 2002)]

Dominion means "supreme authority."

Asperities refers to roughness of manner.

 What do you think of Adams's comments? Write a letter to the former president, telling him your thoughts.

By the mid-1800s, however, some Jews were beginning to think seriously about re-creating a Jewish homeland in Eretz Yisrael, the land of Israel, which by then was part of the Ottoman, or Turkish, Empire. Some Jews thought a homeland was important for religious reasons. Nationalist movements in Europe inspired others. Still others wanted the Jews to have a place to which to escape antisemitism. The pogroms that had devastated the Russian Jewish communities in 1881 convinced many Jews throughout the world that they needed to establish a Jewish homeland. Although some were willing to consider locations other than Palestine, most Jews concluded that Palestine should be the site.

In 1882–1883, outraged by the pogroms, the American Jewish poet, Emma Lazarus wrote a series of letters, "An Epistle to the Hebrews," based on her Zionist ideas. She, too, saw Palestine as a safe haven for persecuted Jews. Some Eastern European pioneers sailed to Palestine to begin a new life there, but most other immigrants made their way to the United States, where some established Zionist organizations that they modeled on similar groups in the Old Country.

An **epistle** is a lengthy letter.

SUPPORT FOR A HOMELAND GROWS

Antisemitism was increasing in western Europe just as it was in Eastern Europe and the United States. The Dreyfus affair, which occurred in France in 1894, especially disturbed Theodor Herzl. Alfred Dreyfus, a Jewish army officer, had been falsely accused of spying for the Germans, and the French government and army hid evidence of his innocence. Herzl witnessed the ceremony in which Dreyfus's medals were ripped from his uniform, and he heard people in the crowd yelling, "Death to the Jews." (Dreyfus, who was exiled to Devil's Island, French Guiana, in disgrace, was finally declared innocent in 1906 and promoted after this.)

Convinced that the only answer to antisemitism was the reestablishment of a Jewish state in Palestine, Herzl wrote Der Judenstaat (The Jewish State), which was published in 1896. The book united people who were interested in Zionist ideas. One year later, he initiated the

Henrietta Szold, at left, at a meeting of the Zionist Provisional Committee in 1915.

First Zionist Congress in Basel, Switzerland, to organize the Zionist movement worldwide. Approximately 200 delegates attended the congress. Although only one American, Rabbi Schepsel Schaffer of Baltimore, was an official delegate, a number of other American Jews were there as observers. Inspired by this dramatic event, more than one hundred Zionist groups in the United States, led by Richard Gottheil, a professor of Semitic languages at Columbia University, formed the Federation of American Zionists (FAZ) the next year.

Other important American Zionist groups formed at about the same time. Hadassah, which began as a small study circle, became a major women's Zionist organization under the leadership of Henrietta Szold. Szold, born in 1860, was the oldest daughter of a well-known Baltimore rabbi. She learned German, French, and Hebrew, and was well educated in Judaism. She was influenced by her father's religious beliefs and by the Zionist poetry of Emma Lazarus. A teacher, writer, and editor, she accepted a full-time position as editor at the Jewish Publication Society in Philadelphia in 1893, although her official job title was secretary. (Scholars have pointed out the gap between her responsibilities and her title.)

After her father's death, Szold and her mother moved to New York, where she joined a women's Zionist group called the Hadassah Study Circle. Members of the group prepared articles on Jewish history and Palestine. While in New York, Szold also became the first woman to take classes in rabbinic studies at the Jewish Theological Seminary, even

The flag of Israel

A little known fact of Jewish history: Jacob Askowith and his son Charles created the Israeli flag in Boston in 1891. The B'nai Zion Educational Society displayed the flag, which had a white background, two horizontal blue stripes, and a magen David ("shield of David") with the name Maccabee written in Hebrew. "Maccabee" was later replaced by "Zion," which was finally dropped as well.

A group of B'nai Zion members carried the flag in a Columbus Day parade in 1892, and _The Boston Globe_ dubbed it the flag of Judah. Isaac Harris of Boston, who attended the First Zionist Congress, brought the flag to the attention of the Zionist movement in 1897. Schepsel Schaffer, a delegate to the congress, may have helped. At the Second Zionist Congress, in 1898, the flag was officially displayed for the first time.

from Jonathan D. Sarna and Ellen Smith, eds., _The Jews of Boston_
(Boston: Combined Jewish Philanthropies, 1995)

DO IT Can you imagine another design for an Israeli flag? Draw it.

though women could not become rabbis at that time.

In 1909, Szold and her mother traveled to Palestine for the first time. Having seen the great need for medical care in the land, Szold's mother suggested that her daughter's study group get involved. On her return, Szold presented this idea to the group, and after nearly two years of preparation she brought them together with other women, hoping to turn her dream into the reality of a national women's Zionist organization. It had the dual goals of Zionist education in America and a specific health-oriented project in Palestine.

The Hadassah chapter of the Daughters of Zion became known as Hadassah, the Women's Zionist Organization of America. It was named in honor of Queen Esther's Hebrew name because it was founded during the week of Purim and because the original study group was known as Hadassah. The organization provided visiting nurses, maternity and dental care, and pasteurized milk to Palestine, and in 1918 sent a pioneer medical unit there. It expanded to include a number of clinics and eventually became the Hadassah Hospital.

Szold moved to Palestine in 1920 to direct the Hadassah medical unit. In the 1930s, as the director of the Youth Aliyah program, she welcomed young Jewish refugees from Nazi Europe. She died in 1945, a few years before the birth of the State of Israel.

DO IT Read about different types of Zionism. With which viewpoint do you agree? Create a poster expressing your point of view.

Henrietta Szold and Palestine

Szold wrote from Jerusalem on March 13, 1921, shortly after she arrived to head Hadassah's medical unit:

from Marvin Lowenthal, *Henrietta Szold: Life and Letters* (New York: Viking Press, 1942)

"I am on the great adventure of my life . . . It seems downright funny for me to be doing medical organization in Jerusalem . . . But what do you think of my riding up one of the steepest mountains strewn with stones, donkeyback, sitting astride? I am so proud of that feat that I can't stop talking about it . . . But . . . the real thing is the gamut of human emotions and reactions . . . and that is hard to describe. . . .

"The Jews are ready to work—and they are working . . . The [workers'] camps are full of faults of organization, the campers full of faults of temperament, but the movement as a whole is a phenomenon equivalent to a miracle. . . .

"And the country? It too is a miracle. Full of faults, like the camp—and the campers, but so beautiful. It too must be conquered, its stones, its climate, its swamps, but it is worth, oh! so worth the struggle. I was sent to Galilee on business four weeks ago. It was raining, raining all the week I was away. Neither clouds, nor mist, nor downpour of abundant waters, nor bad roads could obscure the beauty of the land in its spring garb."

LOOK AT IT

Mark Twain visits the Holy Land

The famous American author, Mark Twain, visited Palestine in 1867. In his book, *Innocents Abroad*, published in 1881, he wrote:

"The further we went, the hotter the sun got, and the more rocky and bare, repulsive and dreary the landscape became. There could not have been more fragments of stone strewn over this part of the world if every ten square feet of the land had been occupied by a separate and distinct stonecutter's establishment for an age. There was hardly a tree or a shrub anywhere. Even the olive and the cactus, those fast friends of a worthless soil, had almost deserted the country. No landscape exists that is more tiresome to the eye than that which bounds the approaches to Jerusalem. The only difference between the roads and the surrounding country, perhaps, is that there are rather more rocks in the roads than in the surrounding country."

Gamut means "range."

THINK ABOUT IT Compare Szold's description of Palestine with Twain's. In your opinion, why were their descriptions so different?

DO IT Have you visited Israel? Did you keep a diary or write letters or postcards home? Have you talked to people about their trips to Israel? Have you seen pictures of the country? Write your own description of the Land of Israel.

DIFFERING OPINIONS

Even as new organizations were founded, the American Jewish community was divided in its opinion of Zionism. Among its supporters was Dr. Solomon Schechter, who became chancellor of the Jewish Theological Seminary in 1902. In a 1906 statement he declared that Zionism would spark renewed interest in Jewish religion and culture. Others, however, were either uninterested in or opposed to the movement. There were those American Jews who were busy earning a living, caring for their families, and becoming part of American society. Some saw Zionism as unnecessary, and others feared that their participation might lead non-Jews to question their loyalty to the United States. Jacob Schiff, the noted philanthropist, said: "Speaking as an American, I cannot for a moment conceive that one can be at the same time a true American and an honest adherent of the Zionist movement." Nonetheless, Schiff gave significant financial support to educational, medical, and agricultural projects in Palestine and later changed his opinion. Some American Jews, fearful of growing antisemitism in the United States, hesitated to support Zionism publicly.

An **adherent** is someone who supports a particular position.

Do you agree with Schiff's early opinion of Zionism? Why or why not?

Orthodox Jews also found themselves divided on the issue of Zionism. Some rejected it out of the belief that the Jews' return to the Holy Land would occur only with the coming of the Messiah. They saw Zionism as a secular movement that would establish a nonreligious society there. Others joined Mizrachi, a religious Zionist organization, hoping that by reestablishing a Jewish homeland they could infuse new energy into religious life in Israel and around the world.

The American Reform movement held a different view. In its 1885 Pittsburgh Platform, the movement took the position that Jews were a religious group, not a nation or a people. After the first Zionist Congress, the CCAR passed a resolution stating: "We totally disapprove of any attempt for the establishment of a Jewish state." It concluded: "No return to Palestine is expected, nor the re-institution there of a Jewish state."

Even so, a number of well-known Reform rabbis, including Gustav Gottheil of Temple Emanu-El in New York, took leadership positions in the Zionist movement. Judah Magnes of New York became the first president of the Hebrew University in Jerusalem. Bernhard Felsenthal of Chicago, who had delivered an antislavery sermon just before the start of the Civil War, supported Zionism publicly. Stephen S. Wise, a founder of the Federation of American Zionists (FAZ), served as the American secretary of the international Zionist Organization.

What do you think of the opinions expressed by some Orthodox and Reform Jews about Zionism?

Many Jewish labor leaders and socialists also did not support Zionism, believing that it was more important to help poor Jews in the United States and other countries than to concentrate their energies on the Land of Israel. Socialists saw Zionism as a bourgeois movement that did not relate to the daily needs of the workers and their families, and they believed that antisemitism could be eliminated only by changing the class system. There were groups of socialist Zionists, however, known as Poale Zion, who accepted a mix of Zionist and socialist theories.

The problems caused by these philosophical disagreements were compounded because the Zionist movement's organizations were weak. The FAZ did not attract much support and suffered from organizational problems. Some Zionist groups never joined it, and others later broke away from it. By the beginning of World War I, when the U.S. Jewish population was more than 2.5 million, the FAZ only had 12,000 members. American Zionism faced a difficult beginning.

Bourgeois refers to the middle class.

You can find information about Zionism online at the Jewish Virtual Library. Go to www.us-israel.org/jsource/zion.html.

CHAPTER 8
AMERICAN ZIONISM GROWS

What were some of the challenges facing Zionism as it developed and expanded its influence in the United States?

Still in its infancy, the American Zionist movement was struggling. Zionist organizations were weak and disorganized, and the movement's leaders disagreed with one another on key issues. Some American Jews doubted that one could be both a loyal American and a good Zionist. One man, Louis Dembitz Brandeis, was largely responsible for convincing people that this was possible.

BRANDEIS MAKES A DIFFERENCE

Louis D. Brandeis

Born in Louisville, Kentucky, in 1856, Louis D. Brandeis graduated from high school with highest honors at age fifteen, studied in Europe, attended Harvard University, and before his twenty-first birthday graduated from its law school at the head of the class. During his early years, an uncle, Lewis Dembitz, an Orthodox Jew whose name he took as his middle name, was a significant influence. Brandeis grew up with little Jewish education, and he began to appreciate his Jewish heritage, as well as Zionist ideas, only as an adult.

Brandeis was a brilliant and successful lawyer whose work for women's rights, to protect consumers, and against monopolies in big business earned him the nickname "the People's Lawyer." His devotion to public causes led to his involvement in Jewish causes. When he helped settle the "Great Revolt"—a strike in the clothing industry in New York in 1910—he learned about the life of the Jewish immigrants on the Lower East Side and began to feel a bond with the workers he met.

At the beginning of World War I, Brandeis agreed to serve as chairman of the Provisional Executive Committee for General Zionist Affairs. This group had formed in 1914 to raise money for Jews in Palestine, who were

suffering on account of blockades and other conditions caused by the war. Brandeis strongly believed that to be good Americans, Jews must be better Jews, and to be better Jews, they must be Zionists. That did not mean, he pointed out, that American Jews had to live in Palestine.

 In **monopolies**, one person or group of people has control over something, such as a product or a service.

 Do you agree that being a good Jew helps you to be a better American and that being a Zionist helps you to be a better Jew? Why or why not?

In 1916, when President Woodrow Wilson appointed Brandeis to the Supreme Court, Brandeis became the country's first Jewish Supreme Court justice, and antisemitism soon surfaced. Brandeis was well respected, however, and enjoyed the support of many Americans. He took his place on the Court and earned a fine reputation.

Brandeis's talent for organization helped him in his work for the Zionist movement. He reorganized the FAZ, in 1918, as the Zionist Organization of America (ZOA). His motto, "Men, Money, Discipline," guided the staff as they created new materials to publicize Zionist activities, employed more effective methods to raise money, and adopted more efficient ways to keep records. Brandeis and his followers wanted the money raised from Jews in the Diaspora to be used to support a new Jewish homeland. They focused on support for Hebrew education and higher education in Palestine, as well as Jewish control of Palestine's natural resources.

 A **diaspora** is a scattering of a people around the world in places other than their homeland. The Jewish Diaspora comprises all settlements of Jews outside the Land of Israel.

 Why was it important that a person as well-known and respected in the United States as Louis Brandeis became involved in the Zionist movement?

 Young Jews get involved: Learn about Zionist youth groups with branches in the United States, such as Young Judea, B'nei Akiva, and Habonim Dror. You can find information on the Internet at www.youngjudea.org, www.bneiakiva.org, and www.habonimdror.org.

AN IMPORTANT DECLARATION

World War I began in Europe in 1914, but the United States did not enter the war until 1917. Throughout the war, discussions had taken place about the establishment of a Jewish homeland in Palestine. In November 1917, with Great Britain about to capture Palestine from the Ottoman Empire, Great Britain's foreign minister, Arthur James Balfour, wrote to Lord Lionel Rothschild, a leader of the Jewish community in England, promising British support for the establishment of a Jewish homeland in Palestine. The letter became known as the Balfour Declaration.

Zionists around the world were delighted, hoping that they would soon create a Jewish state. Zionist activity in America increased, and celebrations were held in many cities. About 2,700 American Jews joined the Jewish Legion, the Jewish military units formed to support British troops in Palestine during World War I. Justice Brandeis and Rabbi Stephen S. Wise played major roles in persuading President Wilson to support the declaration. At the

Paris Peace Conference following the war, a number of well-known American Zionists, who were part of the Jewish delegation, explained why a Jewish homeland in Palestine was necessary.

As a result of the involvement of Louis Brandeis, more efficient organization, and the excitement caused by the Balfour Declaration, greater numbers of American Jews were attracted to Zionism. By 1919, the ZOA had about 140,000 members. Even though Britain backed away from the Balfour Declaration in 1920 and accepted a mandate to oversee Palestine, the proposal helped the Zionists' cause. One major disappointment was the 1922 British decision to award a significant part of Palestine to the Arabs to form the nation of Transjordan.

 A **mandate** is the legal responsibility to carry out a program or policy. Under the League of Nations, it specifically referred to a member nation's responsibility for a territory.

The "Joint"

The American Jewish Joint Distribution Committee was organized in 1914 to enlist Eastern European Jews, German Jews, and Jewish socialists to aid Jews around the world. It also brought together Orthodox, Reform, and secular Jews. The "Joint," as the organization is known, raised $15 million during World War I for medical assistance, food, and clothes for refugees in Europe and for the yishuv in Palestine. After World War II, it provided assistance to refugees who fled the pogroms in Russia and Poland. When the Nazis came to power, it helped 180,000 Jews escape from Europe, and it later came to the aid of Jewish survivors. After the war, the "Joint" became more sympathetic to Zionism, helping to organize illegal immigration to Palestine and supporting the immigrants whom the British had sent to displaced persons camps in Cyprus.

 Yishuv refers to the Jewish settlement in Palestine. It comes from the Hebrew root *yud, shin, bet* meaning "to sit," or "to stay."

Displaced persons (DPs) are refugees forced to leave their country on account of war or oppression.

A significant letter

The Balfour Declaration approved by the British government, stated:

"I have much pleasure in conveying to you, on behalf of His Majesty's Government, the following declaration of sympathy with Jewish Zionist aspirations which has been submitted to, and approved by, the Cabinet:

"His Majesty's Government views with favour the establishment in Palestine of a national home for the Jewish people, and will use their best endeavours to facilitate the achievement of this object, it being clearly understood that nothing shall be done which may prejudice the civil and religious rights of existing non-Jewish communities in Palestine, or the rights and political status enjoyed by Jews in any other country.'

"I should be grateful if you would bring this declaration to the knowledge of the Zionist Federation."

DO IT If you had been alive in 1919, would you have been a Zionist? Why or why not? Are you a Zionist today? Explain.

Learn about the following Jewish organizations: the Zionist Organization of America on the Internet at www.zoa.org and the American Jewish Congress at www.americanjewishcongress.org.

A TIME OF CONTRADICTIONS

Despite the enthusiasm produced by the Balfour Declaration, membership in the ZOA began to decline in the 1920s. Antisemitism was increasing, and some American Jews worried about their own position in American society, fearing that they would be viewed as unpatriotic. With fewer members and other Jewish organizations competing for donations, the ZOA had difficulty raising money.

At the same time, groups within the Zionist movement were in disagreement. One group, led by Brandeis, wanted to build Palestine in practical, typically American business-like ways. The other group was more interested in spreading Zionist ideals and culture and furthering the establishment of socialist kibbutzim. This faction was led by Chaim Weizmann, who was president of the international Zionist Organization (later called the World Zionist Organization or WZO). The two groups disagreed not just on these basic goals but on ways of raising money for Palestine and distributing it there. At the ZOA convention in 1921, for a variety of personal and organizational reasons, Brandeis's group resigned, and Weizmann's group took control, although some of those who resigned did return to the group's leadership later.

Although the ZOA was not managed efficiently in the 1920s, many positive developments were taking place in American Zionism. Several leading American Jews, some of whom were rabbis, strongly supported the Zionist cause. Rabbi Stephen S. Wise, who was active in both the FAZ and the ZOA, made Zionism a key part of the program of the American Jewish Congress, which he and other Jewish leaders founded in 1918 in response to the conditions of European Jews following World War I. Although fund-raising was difficult, several groups united in 1925 under Wise's leadership to form a fund-raising organization called the United Palestine Appeal. Prominent Reform Rabbi Abba Hillel Silver, a vehement supporter of Zionism, discussed Zionism in speeches he gave around the country, and Rabbi Mordecai Kaplan, a leading American Jewish thinker, lectured widely and wrote several influential articles and books on the subject.

A number of important American Jews went to live in Palestine and took leadership roles in the yishuv. Henrietta Szold settled there in 1920 to lead the Hadassah medical unit and Rabbi Judah Magnes emigrated in 1922, later serving as the first president of Hebrew University. Perhaps the most famous American to emigrate was Golda Mabovitz Meyerson. Meyerson moved from Milwaukee to Palestine in 1921, settled on Kibbutz Merhavia, later changed her name to Meir, and served as the prime minister of Israel.

Kibbutzim are collective Jewish farms. Property is owned by the entire kibbutz. Work and governing the kibbutz are shared by the collective's members. While the pioneering settlements were agricultural, today many produce industrial goods.

Find out about the lives of Stephen S. Wise, Abba Hillel Silver, or Mordecai Kaplan.

DECISIONS ARE MADE

Some important American Jews who did not support political Zionism now joined the Jewish Agency, the group that governed the yishuv. Over the years, they had begun to appreciate the importance of Israel and the work of its settlers, and they cooperated with the Zionists on various agricultural, educational, and charitable projects in Palestine.

Almost as soon as the Balfour Declaration was issued, the Arab world responded with violence. In 1929, Arabs murdered sixty-eight people in the Jewish quarter of Hebron, seventeen Jews in Jerusalem, and twenty in the Jewish quarter of Safed. Jewish settlements throughout Palestine were attacked, and some had to be abandoned. The "disturbances" of 1929 took the lives of 133 people, and another 339 were hurt when the British authorities did little to stop the riots. Around the world, Jews united in increasing numbers to support the yishuv as they recognized the strength of Arab nationalism in Palestine and the widespread Arab opposition to a Jewish homeland.

Nationalism in this context refers to a devotion to the interests of a nation and advocacy of the advancement and/or the independence of that nation.

Why was it important for non-Zionists to support the Jewish Agency? Do you support Israel? Why or why not? If so, what do you do? Make a list.

Golda

David Ben-Gurion, first Prime Minister of Israel, and Golda Meir.

Golda Mabovitch was born in Kiev, Russia, in 1898 and came with her family to the United States in 1906. As a young girl in Russia, she learned about Zionism from her older sister, who met in secret with Jews who were planning to escape that country's antisemitism. As a young woman, Meir taught school in Milwaukee. She married Morris Meyerson in 1917, but was not happy with the life of a housewife and insisted that they immigrate to Palestine. In 1921, they settled on Kibbutz Merhavia, and Golda soon became active in Labor Zionism.

Meir wrote about her experience on Kibbutz Merhavyah in her autobiography, *My Life*:

"On Friday evenings it was customary for the kibbutzniks to change: The men put on clean shirts, and the girls wore skirts and blouses instead of work dresses or pants. But I couldn't see the logic of once-a-week neatness. I didn't care what I wore every day, but it had to be ironed. Every night, using a heavy iron heated by coal, I religiously pressed my 'sack,' knowing that the kibbutzniks not only thought I was mad, but also suspected me of not being a true pioneer at heart. There was similar disapproval about the flower design that Morris painted on the walls of our room so that it would look nicer, to say nothing of the fuss about the crates he painted and turned into cupboards for us. It took quite a while, in fact, for the kibbutz to accept our strange 'American' ways and us."

Meir served as Israel's minister of labor from 1949 to 1956 and as minister of foreign affairs from 1956 to 1966. She became prime minister of Israel in 1969 and resigned in 1974 after critics claimed that her government had been ill prepared for the 1973 Yom Kippur War. She died in 1978.

CHAPTER 9
TOWARD STATEHOOD

What effect did the events surrounding World War II have on Zionism in America?

With the rise of Nazism, American Jews wanted to support the Jews of Europe. They understood the importance of Palestine as a home for Jews fleeing Nazi oppression, and as restrictions on U.S. immigration increased, they realized that fewer Jews would be permitted to immigrate to the United States. Even some Jews who had not been Zionists were changing their minds.

SUPPORT FOR ZIONISM BUILDS

In its early days, the Reform movement opposed Zionism. As time went on, however, more Jews of Eastern Europe background joined the movement. Many of them were Zionists, and they influenced the movement's leadership and its view of Zionism. In 1935, Rabbi Felix Levy, a strong Zionist, was elected president of the Central Conference of American Rabbis (CCAR) and under his influence, at a meeting in Columbus, Ohio, in 1937, the organization officially changed its position on Zionism. Included in the Columbus Platform, a general statement of principles, was a declaration that all Jews must help make Palestine a safe Jewish homeland for Jews who were oppressed and a center for Jewish culture and religion.

 Do you agree that all Jews—even those in the United States—should have been obligated to help create a Jewish homeland in Palestine? Why or why not? Was the Nazis' persecution of the Jews a valid reason for creating a Jewish homeland?

American Jews were angry at British policies regarding Palestine, especially after the White Paper of May 1939 strictly limited the number of Jews who could immigrate to the yishuv and restricted the sale of land in Palestine to Jewish settlers. Large demonstrations were organized to protest the White Paper, which was seen as a betrayal of the Balfour Declaration. By this time, membership in

Zionist organizations like the ZOA and Hadassah had increased. American Jews were also giving much-needed money to Zionist causes, especially through the United Jewish Appeal (UJA).

Nonetheless, Zionist groups disagreed among themselves, and Zionists and non-Zionists continued to disagree about rescue strategies, hindering the efforts of the American Jewish community to help the European refugees. While many Zionists saw Palestine as the Jewish homeland and the best haven for the refugees, other Jewish leaders believed it was important to explore different ways to rescue Europe's Jews.

By the early 1940s, the horrors of the Holocaust had become known. Even non-Zionist leaders, like those who directed the American Jewish Committee, were ready to work with the Zionists to establish a Jewish homeland in Palestine. In June 1941, they signed commitments favoring the continuation of Jewish rights under the British mandate and the fulfillment of the Balfour Declaration. They hoped that unrestricted Jewish immigration to, and settlement in, Palestine would result in a Jewish majority and a national homeland.

 A **White Paper** is a government report on a subject. In 1922, 1931, and 1939, the British government issued White Papers that interpreted the Balfour Declaration.

Great Britain's Division of the Mandated Area: Palestine and Transjordan after 1922

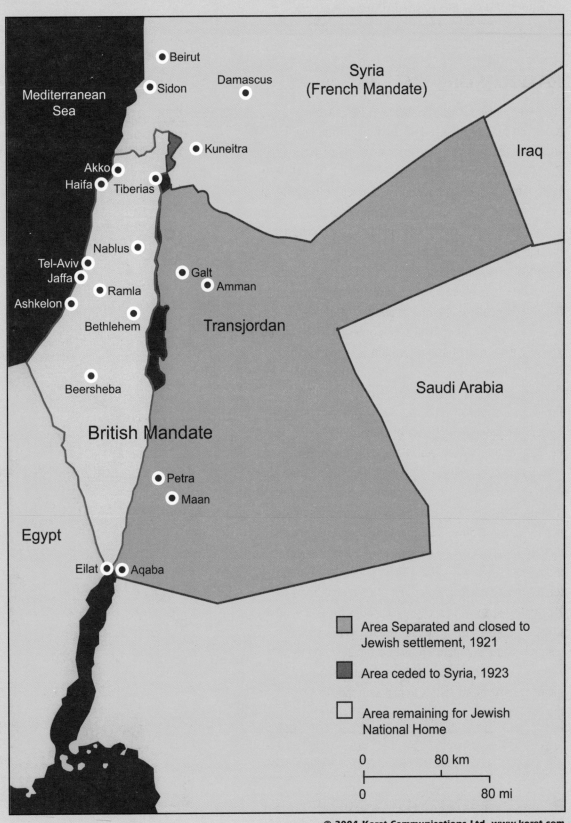

Beirut

Sidon

Damascus

Mediterranean Sea

Syria (French Mandate)

Iraq

Kuneitra

Akko

Haifa

Tiberias

Nablus

Tel-Aviv

Jaffa

Galt

Amman

Ramla

Ashkelon

Bethlehem

Transjordan

Saudi Arabia

Beersheba

British Mandate

Petra

Maan

Egypt

Eilat

Aqaba

Area Separated and closed to Jewish settlement, 1921

Area ceded to Syria, 1923

Area remaining for Jewish National Home

0   80 km

0   80 mi

© 2004 Koret Communications Ltd. www.koret.com

To see a campaign letter from a 1947 UJA fund-raising drive, visit the website of the Jewish Women's Archive, at www.jwa.org/teach/primarysources.

PASSION GROWS

Pro-Zionist feelings continued to build among American Jews as the need for a refuge for the Jewish victims of the Nazis became even more obvious and as the British continued to limit Jewish immigration to Palestine. Rabbi Abba Hillel Silver encouraged much of the political organizing by American Jews who supported a Jewish state in Palestine. In his view, "The upbuilding of a Jewish national home in Palestine is one great, urgent, and historically inescapable task of Jewry. The upbuilding of Jewish religious life in America and elsewhere throughout the world, inclusive of Israel, is another. One is no substitute for the other. One is not opposed to the other."

At a gathering of American Zionist leaders at the Biltmore Hotel in New York City in May 1942, 600 delegates passed a resolution. Known as the Biltmore Program, it supported the creation of a Jewish military force, demanded that control of immigration to Palestine be given to the Jewish Agency, and called for the establishment of a sovereign Jewish state in Palestine after the war. A year later, another conference of delegates from a variety of American Jewish organizations took place. At Rabbi Silver's urging, the delegates expressed their support for the establishment of a Jewish state in Palestine. Silver argued: "There is but one solution for national homelessness. That is a national home." He organized some of the Zionist groups formed before the war into the American Zionist Emergency Council, which became the main group coordinating American Zionists' lobbying efforts. Throughout the war, members organized rallies to maintain awareness of the Zionist cause.

A **lobby** is a group of private individuals who try to influence government policy.

Look at these posters advertising the Land of Israel. Make a poster that will persuade pioneers to go to the land. Use one of the following famous quotations about Zion and Jerusalem, or find one that inspires you.

- Awake, awake, O Zion! Clothe yourself in your strength; dress yourself in the clothes of your Jerusalem, the holy city. (Isaiah 52:1)

- For learning shall come forth from Zion, the word of God from Jerusalem. (Isaiah 2:3)

- There shall yet old men and old women sit in the squares of Jerusalem . . . and the broad places of the city shall be crowded with boys and girls playing. (Zechariah 8:4–5)]

DO IT

Debate the issue. The question is whether a Jewish homeland should be established in Palestine. Which side will you take? Why? Prepare your arguments on a separate sheet of paper.

At this time, American Zionist leaders were worried that President Franklin D. Roosevelt's backing of the Zionist cause had weakened, and they attempted to maintain his support. Bipartisan resolutions were proposed in Congress, which initially favored the establishment of a Jewish state in Palestine. There were, however, those who opposed this goal. When the resolutions finally passed in December 1945, they contained no mention of a Jewish state, although they supported free Jewish immigration to Palestine.

Bipartisan means "including or representing members of two political parties."

A NEW PRESIDENT LENDS SUPPORT

Roosevelt died in office in 1945, and Vice President Harry Truman became president. Truman showed concern for the Jewish refugees crowded into DP camps in Europe and permitted many of them to immigrate to the United States. He also favored allowing a large number of European Jewish refugees to settle in Palestine immediately. Because of pressure from the Arabs, the British had continued to restrict Jewish immigration. In November 1945, the Anglo-American Committee of Inquiry was formed to explore solutions to the problem. It recommended that 100,000 European Jews be allowed to enter Palestine but opposed the creation of a Jewish state. Instead, it proposed setting up a United Nations trusteeship and, later, a binational state. Britain rejected this plan.

Support for partition began to build. With increasing violence between Arabs, Jews, and the British in Palestine, Great Britain turned the problem over to the newly created United Nations, and the UN Special Committee on Palestine was formed. Investigations were held in Europe and Palestine. The committee's majority report recommended the establishment of two states—one Jewish and one Arab—with economic ties between them. It also proposed that Jerusalem remain under international rule. The General Assembly debated the plan, and on November 29, by a vote of thirty-three to thirteen with ten countries abstaining and one absent, voted for partition. The Zionists accepted the plan, although it gave them very little land. The Arabs rejected it. The leaders of the Jewish Agency in Palestine decided to declare Israel a state on May 14, 1948, the day the British were scheduled to depart. The armies of six Arab countries—Egypt, Syria, Jordan, Iraq, Saudi Arabia, and Lebanon—prepared to invade.

LEARN IT

Anglo means "English."

In a **trusteeship** a group of individuals is appointed to administer the affairs of a territory.

Partition is the division of a country into two or more separate political units. Here it refers to the division of Palestine into two states, one Arab and one Jewish.

THINK ABOUT IT

What is your opinion of the proposal to establish two states—one Jewish and one Arab—and establish international rule over Jerusalem? How might the situation be different today had this plan been accepted by the Arabs?

American Jewish leaders hoped to enlist political support for Palestine and help European refugees immigrate. They appealed to President Truman and

U.N. Partition of Palestine, 1947

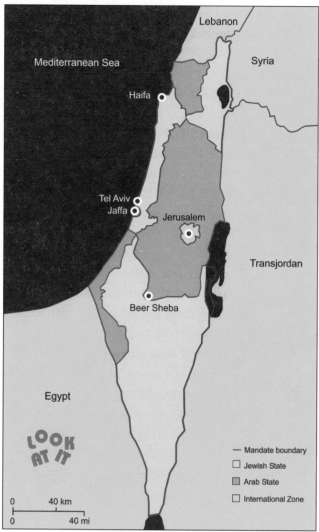

© 2004 Koret Communications Ltd. www.koret.com

concerned about the refugees. In the days before the British mandate expired, he discussed the situation with his aides. When David Ben-Gurion, chairman of the Jewish Agency's Executive Committee, read Israel's Declaration of Independence on May 14, 1948, Truman responded within a few hours, becoming the first world leader to recognize the State of Israel.

 Read Israel's Declaration of Independence by clicking on www.yale.edu/lawweb/ Avalon/mideast/Israel.htm. To read the U.S. Declaration of Independence, visit www.archives.gov/national_archives_ experience/declaration.

DO IT

What are some of the most important points of Israel's Declaration of Independence? Compare it with the American Declaration of Independence. What are some significant similarities and differences?

Congress but were opposed by officials in the State Department who did not wish to challenge either the British or the Arabs. The State Department's concerns centered on three major issues: economic repercussions because of U.S. dependence on Arab oil, military problems because the Middle East was an important area strategically, and the prospect of religious conflict because of the presence of Christian missionaries and Muslim shrines in the Holy Land. Zionists, who wanted Truman to persuade the British to open Palestine to free Jewish immigration, flooded the White House with demands that he support partition.

Once it was obvious that the yishuv's leaders would declare a state regardless of the consequences, Zionists lobbied for Truman's recognition of the new state. Although Truman seemed annoyed by the pressure, he remained

AMERICANS HELP IN OTHER WAYS

American Jews raised large amounts of money for the Zionist cause, contributing to organizations like Hadassah and responding to UJA campaigns. After the war, Golda Meir was one of several Israeli leaders who traveled through the United States to raise funds for the UJA. Meir's speeches were so powerful that she moved some listeners to tears. Some borrowed money from banks in order to make immediate gifts to Palestine.

In a fund-raising speech, in January 1948, before an American Jewish audience in Chicago, Meir declared: "The Jewish community in Palestine is going to fight to the very end. If we have arms to fight with, we will fight with them. If not, we will fight with stones in our hands. . . . if these seven hundred thousand Jews in Palestine can remain alive, then the Jewish people as such is alive. . . . You cannot decide whether we should fight or not. We will. The Jewish community in Palestine will raise no white flag for the mufti. That decision is taken. Nobody can change it. You can only decide one thing: whether we shall be victorious in this fight or whether the mufti will be victorious. That decision American Jews can make. It has to be made quickly, within hours, within days. And I beg of you—don't be too late. Don't be bitterly sorry three months from now for what you failed to do today. The time is now." [from Golda Meir, *My Life* (Jerusalem: Steinmatzky, 1975)]

A **mufti** is an interpreter of Muslim religious law.

If you had been in Golda Meir's audience, how might you have reacted? Can Meir's words be applied to today's relationship between American Jews and Israel?

A famous floating symbol

To stop illegal immigration, Great Britain issued a policy whereby ships carrying unauthorized immigrants would be sent back to the ports in Europe from which they had sailed. The first ship to which it applied the policy was the *Exodus* 1947. The *Exodus* sailed from a port near Marseilles, France, on July 11, 1947, with 4,515 immigrants, including 655 children, on board. British destroyers accompanied it as soon as it left French waters. On July 18, near the coast of Palestine, the British rammed the ship and boarded it. The immigrants on board fought desperately, but two passengers and a crewman were killed, and thirty people were injured. The ship was towed to Haifa, and the passengers were forced onto ships that would return them to France.

On reaching a port in southern France, the immigrants refused to leave the ship, remaining in the ship's holds for twenty-four days, despite a heat wave, a shortage of food, overcrowding, and poor sanitary conditions. The French government refused to force them off the ship. Finally, the British instructed the ship to sail for Germany. There, the immigrants were forced off the ship and taken to detention camps.

When journalists reported the story, people throughout the world were outraged. In response, the British changed their policy, taking the immigrants to detention camps on Cyprus, an island off the coast of Turkey, rather than sending them back to Europe.

Most of the passengers on the *Exodus* finally succeeded in immigrating, although some had to wait until after the State of Israel was established.

Would you have stayed on the *Exodus* given the poor conditions on board?

The author Leon Uris told the story of the *Exodus* in a well-known book by that name. Read the book or see the 1960 movie and compare these versions to the historical account.

DO IT

The contributions made by American Jews went to support DPs, including illegal immigrants, settling in Palestine. Once Israel's War of Independence began, American Jews quietly raised funds for the purchase and shipment of supplies crucial to the war effort, including scrap metal, arms, warplanes, and ships that would carry illegal immigrants.

About 3,500 volunteers from thirty-seven countries, including the United States, came to Israel's side. Both Jews and non-Jews joined a special force called MACHAL (from the Hebrew *Mitnadvei Chutz L'Aretz,* Volunteers from Outside the Land of Israel), organized to help the new Israeli army. Probably the most famous of the volunteers was David "Mickey" Marcus, a graduate of the U.S. military academy at West Point, who had served in the American army in World War II. After the war, he continued to work with the army in Europe and met many survivors of the Holocaust. He became convinced that their only hope was a Jewish homeland in Palestine, and

he volunteered to help. The U.S. War Department permitted him to do so as long as he did not use his own name or rank.

"Mickey Stone" arrived in Tel Aviv and took command of the Jerusalem front, helping to turn new Israeli soldiers into an efficient fighting force. When the Jewish section of Jerusalem was about to fall to the Arabs, he ordered the building of the famous "Burma Road," which bypassed Arab blockades to bring supplies into the city. He was the first officer to receive the new rank of *aluf* (brigadier general) in the Israeli army. Sadly, Marcus did not live to see peace. On the night of June 11, 1948, six hours before the fighting stopped, he was unable to sleep. Wrapped in his bedsheet, he walked outside the fence of his headquarters in Abu Ghosh. A guard, thinking him an Arab, shot him dead. He was buried with military honors at West Point, and on his tombstone are the words "A Soldier for All Humanity." The Israeli village of Mishmar David is named for him.

Another American in MACHAL was Al Schwimmer, an airline flight engineer and pilot who volunteered to help the Israeli Air Force (IAF) by buying planes and recruiting airmen in the United States. He also played an important role in organizing the IAF Air Transport Command. Paul Shulman, a U.S. Naval Academy graduate, had fought in the Pacific during World War II. His parents were Zionists, and in 1947 he resigned from the navy and immigrated to Israel. At David Ben-Gurion's request, he helped organize Israel's navy. He was later appointed commander. When Shulman learned that two Egyptian warships were anchored just outside Tel Aviv harbor, he organized an attack force, sinking the flagship of the Egyptian navy in what was Israel's most important naval victory of the War of Independence. After the war, Shulman became an Israeli citizen.

Semisecret military help from the United States

Beginning in 1945, $8 million was raised in only six months for secret operations whose purpose was to buy machinery and blueprints in order to produce weapons for Jews planning to fight for independence in Palestine. By the end of 1948 about fifty military planes had been flown or shipped in crates to Israel.

DO IT See the 1966 movie *Cast a Giant Shadow*, with Kirk Douglas as Mickey Marcus.

THINK ABOUT IT Think about Justice Brandeis's remarks about being a good Jew and a good American. Do you think that Mickey Marcus, Al Schwimmer, Paul Shulman, and the other Americans who fought for Israel were good Americans and good Jews?

DO IT

Personal history: Ask your grandparents, teachers, or adult friends what they remember about this important time in Jewish history. Where were they, and what were they doing, when Israel declared its independence? Did they participate in any Zionist activities? Record your interviews on audiotape or video.

David "Mickey" Marcus

FINALLY, STATEHOOD

Many Jews in the United States and around the world greeted Israel's proclamation of independence with joy. They sang *Hatikvah* ("The Hope"), the new state's national anthem, and danced the *hora* in the streets. Most Jews in America felt strong ties to the Jews in Israel. They also felt that they had played an important part in the birth of the new state. Over the years, Zionism had deeply affected Jewish life in the United States. It had given American Jews a sense of mission and had strengthened their feelings of Jewish peoplehood.

DO IT **Notable Zionists**

Unscramble the names of these well-known Zionists you read about in Unit 3, and match them with their descriptions.

____ 1. IREM _ _ _ _

____ 2. RIVSLE _ _ _ _ _ _

____ 3. AMSURC _ _ _ _ _ _

____ 4. EISW _ _ _ _

____ 5. GESAMN _ _ _ _ _ _

____ 6. ZSLDO _ _ _ _ _

____ 7. HANO _ _ _ _

____ 8. NADBISRE _ _ _ _ _ _ _ _

____ 9. HECRTCEHS _ _ _ _ _ _ _ _ _

a. Commander of the Jerusalem front during the War of Independence

b. Prime Minister of Israel

c. Head of the Jewish Theological Seminary

d. Founder of Ararat

e. First president of the Hebrew University

f. Reform rabbi behind much of the political organizing by American Jewish Zionists

g. Founder of Hadassah

h. A founder of the Federation of American Zionists and the American Zionist Congress

i. First Jew on the U.S. Supreme Court

Ask your teacher to check your answers in the Teaching Guide.

UNIT 3 TIME LINE OF HISTORICAL EVENTS:
AMERICAN JEWS AND ZIONISM

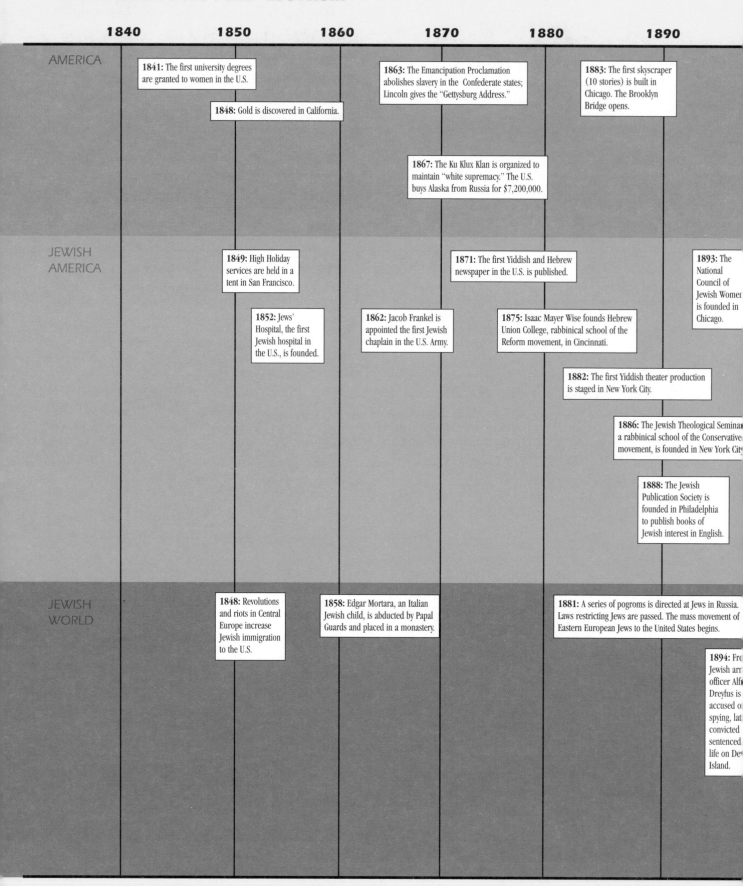

	1840	1850	1860	1870	1880	1890

AMERICA

1841: The first university degrees are granted to women in the U.S.

1848: Gold is discovered in California.

1863: The Emancipation Proclamation abolishes slavery in the Confederate states; Lincoln gives the "Gettysburg Address."

1883: The first skyscraper (10 stories) is built in Chicago. The Brooklyn Bridge opens.

1867: The Ku Klux Klan is organized to maintain "white supremacy." The U.S. buys Alaska from Russia for $7,200,000.

JEWISH AMERICA

1849: High Holiday services are held in a tent in San Francisco.

1871: The first Yiddish and Hebrew newspaper in the U.S. is published.

1893: The National Council of Jewish Women is founded in Chicago.

1852: Jews' Hospital, the first Jewish hospital in the U.S., is founded.

1862: Jacob Frankel is appointed the first Jewish chaplain in the U.S. Army.

1875: Isaac Mayer Wise founds Hebrew Union College, rabbinical school of the Reform movement, in Cincinnati.

1882: The first Yiddish theater production is staged in New York City.

1886: The Jewish Theological Seminary, a rabbinical school of the Conservative movement, is founded in New York City.

1888: The Jewish Publication Society is founded in Philadelphia to publish books of Jewish interest in English.

JEWISH WORLD

1848: Revolutions and riots in Central Europe increase Jewish immigration to the U.S.

1858: Edgar Mortara, an Italian Jewish child, is abducted by Papal Guards and placed in a monastery.

1881: A series of pogroms is directed at Jews in Russia. Laws restricting Jews are passed. The mass movement of Eastern European Jews to the United States begins.

1894: French Jewish army officer Alfred Dreyfus is accused of spying, later convicted and sentenced to life on Devil's Island.

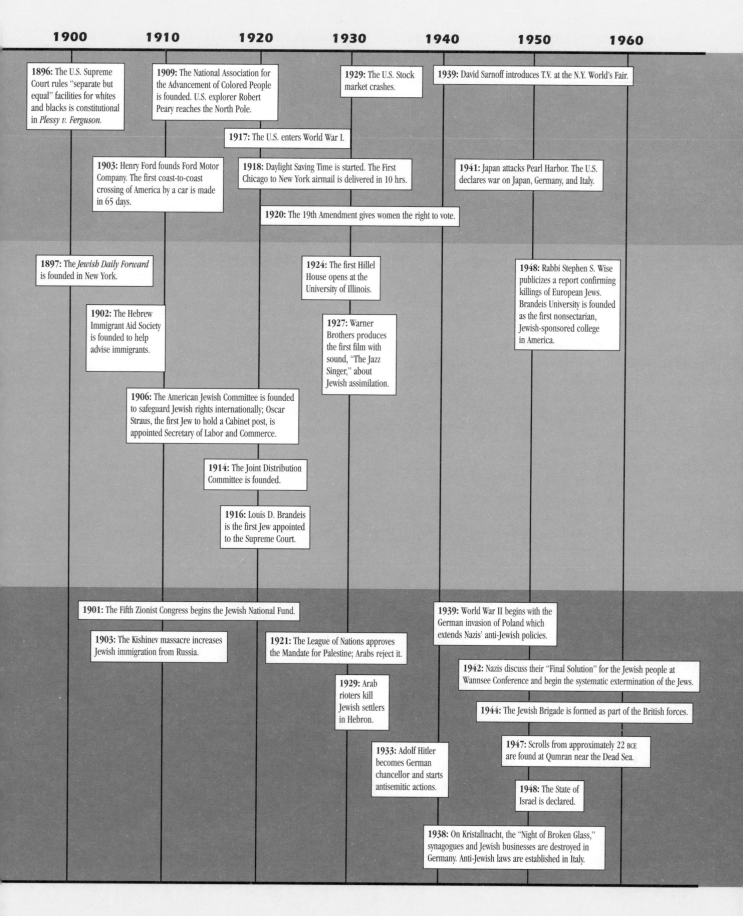

1900   **1910**   **1920**   **1930**   **1940**   **1950**   **1960**

1896: The U.S. Supreme Court rules "separate but equal" facilities for whites and blacks is constitutional in *Plessy v. Ferguson.*

1909: The National Association for the Advancement of Colored People is founded. U.S. explorer Robert Peary reaches the North Pole.

1929: The U.S. Stock market crashes.

1939: David Sarnoff introduces T.V. at the N.Y. World's Fair.

1917: The U.S. enters World War I.

1903: Henry Ford founds Ford Motor Company. The first coast-to-coast crossing of America by a car is made in 65 days.

1918: Daylight Saving Time is started. The First Chicago to New York airmail is delivered in 10 hrs.

1941: Japan attacks Pearl Harbor. The U.S. declares war on Japan, Germany, and Italy.

1920: The 19th Amendment gives women the right to vote.

1897: The *Jewish Daily Forward* is founded in New York.

1924: The first Hillel House opens at the University of Illinois.

1948: Rabbi Stephen S. Wise publicizes a report confirming killings of European Jews. Brandeis University is founded as the first nonsectarian, Jewish-sponsored college in America.

1902: The Hebrew Immigrant Aid Society is founded to help advise immigrants.

1927: Warner Brothers produces the first film with sound, "The Jazz Singer," about Jewish assimilation.

1906: The American Jewish Committee is founded to safeguard Jewish rights internationally; Oscar Straus, the first Jew to hold a Cabinet post, is appointed Secretary of Labor and Commerce.

1914: The Joint Distribution Committee is founded.

1916: Louis D. Brandeis is the first Jew appointed to the Supreme Court.

1901: The Fifth Zionist Congress begins the Jewish National Fund.

1939: World War II begins with the German invasion of Poland which extends Nazis' anti-Jewish policies.

1903: The Kishinev massacre increases Jewish immigration from Russia.

1921: The League of Nations approves the Mandate for Palestine; Arabs reject it.

1942: Nazis discuss their "Final Solution" for the Jewish people at Wannsee Conference and begin the systematic extermination of the Jews.

1929: Arab rioters kill Jewish settlers in Hebron.

1944: The Jewish Brigade is formed as part of the British forces.

1947: Scrolls from approximately 22 BCE are found at Qumran near the Dead Sea.

1933: Adolf Hitler becomes German chancellor and starts antisemitic actions.

1948: The State of Israel is declared.

1938: On Kristallnacht, the "Night of Broken Glass," synagogues and Jewish businesses are destroyed in Germany. Anti-Jewish laws are established in Italy.

THE CURRICULUM DEVELOPMENT TEAM

Shelley Kapnek Rosenberg, Ed.D.

Dr. Shelley Kapnek Rosenberg is the author of *Raising a Mensch: How to Bring Up Ethical Children in Today's World,* (2003) and *Adoption and the Jewish Family: Contemporary Perspectives* (1998). Dr. Rosenberg earned her Ed.D. in psychoeducational processes from Temple University. Since 1994, she has worked for the Auerbach Central Agency for Jewish Education.

Alice L. George, Ph.D.

After twenty years as an editor at newspapers such as the *Detroit Free Press* and the *Philadelphia Daily News,* Alice L. George left journalism to earn a Ph.D. in history at Temple University, which she received in 2001. Her award-winning doctoral dissertation has been turned into a book, *Awaiting Armageddon: How Americans Faced the Cuban Missile Crisis* (2003).

Dianne C. Ashton, Ph.D.

Dianne Ashton is Professor of Religion and Director of the American Studies Program at Rowan University. Her books include *Rebecca Gratz: Women and Judaism in Antebellum America, Jewish Life in Pennsylvania,* and *Four Centuries of Jewish Women's Spirituality.* She publishes widely on American Jewish women.

Reena Sigman Friedman, Ph.D.

Dr. Reena Sigman Friedman is Associate Professor of Modern Jewish Civilization at the Reconstructionist Rabbinical College. She is the author of *These Are Our Children: Jewish Orphanages in the United States, 1880–1925* (1994) and numerous articles and publications. Dr. Friedman is also a faculty member of the Florence Melton Adult Mini-School.

Jonathan D. Sarna, Ph.D.

Jonathan D. Sarna is the Joseph H. and Belle R. Braun Professor of American Jewish History at Brandeis University. Dr. Sarna has written, edited, or co-edited twenty books. Articles, reviews, and commentaries by Dr. Sarna appear regularly in scholarly and popular journals, as well as in Jewish newspapers across North America. He is the author of *American Judaism: A History* (2004).

Nancy M. Messinger

Nancy Messinger has been the Director of Educational Resources at the Auerbach Central Agency for Jewish Education since 1987. She is also the website coordinator for www.acaje.org. Ms. Messinger earned a B.H.L. from the Jewish Theological Seminary, a certificate of Jewish librarianship from Gratz College, a B.S. in history from Columbia University, and an M.S. in counseling from Villanova University.

Rochelle Buller Rabeeya

Rochelle Rabeeya is the Director of Educational Services at the Auerbach Central Agency for Jewish Education. She holds an M.A. and an honorary doctorate in Jewish education from Hebrew Union College–Jewish Institute of Religion and has done post-graduate studies in educational psychology. At ACAJE, she focuses on training school committees, helping schools develop a systemic approach to Jewish education, developing curriculums and coordinating staff development.

Helene Z. Tigay

Helene Z. Tigay has been the Executive Director of the Auerbach Central Agency for Jewish Education since 1990. She has a B.S. in psychology from Columbia University, a B.R.E. in Hebrew literature from the University of Pennsylvania, and has been in the doctoral program in psychological services at the University of Pennsylvania's Graduate School of Education. She has written articles on a variety of topics and is a recipient of the United Synagogue of Conservative Judaism's Ateret Kavod Award.

Julia Prymak

Julia Prymak is the owner of Pryme Design, a graphic design and production services company that manages all aspects of clients' print and promotional needs. She earned her B.F.A. from Rochester Institute of Technology.

Nancy Isserman

Nancy Isserman is the Director of the Challenge and Change: American Jewish History Curriculum Project, and the Associate Director of the Feinstein Center for American Jewish History at Temple University, where she has been since 1992. She is currently working on her dissertation on the determinants of political tolerance in Holocaust survivors at the Graduate Center, City University of New York. She holds an M.S.W. from the George Warren Brown School of Social Work at Washington University.

Murray Friedman, Ph.D.

Dr. Friedman has been the Director of the Feinstein Center for American Jewish History at Temple University since its inception in 1990. He is Director Emeritus of the Philadelphia Chapter of the American Jewish Committee, where he worked for forty-three years. He was vice chairman of the U.S. Commission on Civil Rights from 1986–1989. Dr. Friedman received his Ph.D. from Georgetown University, in American political and social history. He has written numerous articles and books on American Jewish history.